Bench Magazine
Guide to Shop Management

A Compilation of 34 Articles

By 8 Master Jewelers

Arranged Into 6 Categories

This publication is designed to provide competent and reliable information regarding the subject matters covered. However, it is distributed with the understanding that the authors and publishers are not engaged in rendering legal, financial, or other professional advice. Laws and practices often vary from state to state and if legal or other expert assistance is required, the services of a professional should be sought. The authors and publisher specifically disclaim any liability that is incurred from the use or application of the contents of this book.

Warning: Some of the procedures described in this book use sharp and motorized tools and can be harmful if not executed properly. Neither the authors nor the publisher assumes any liability for personal injury resulting from the information presented. Learn about the hazards of all techniques, tools, and materials before using them. Always wear protective goggles and use proper safety measures. Your Safety is Your Responsibility.

Copyrighted 1999 - 2020

Bench Media LLC

Reproduction or translation of any part of this work by any means electronic or mechanical, including photocopying, beyond that permitted by the Copyright Law, without the permission of the publisher, is unlawful.

Welcome to BENCH Magazine

Do you know how many jewelers it takes to change a light bulb?
It takes three!
One to change the light bulb, and two to hold up a screen so that nobody sees the technique used.

Sadly, that joke too closely represents much of our industry. Many master craftsmen go through their careers cautiously guarding their "Trade Secrets" afraid the "competition" would get a leg up on them if they shared their knowledge. As a result, the industry has suffered with far too few skilled workers with the knowledge to perfect their craft.

When I started in this industry in the mid 70's I worked by myself in the shop of a retail store. On occasion, the storeowner would call me downstairs to the store and explain to me that my work was not up to his standards. Not being a bench jeweler himself, he could not explain to me how to improve my work, but he would show me a piece of jewelry from the case and show me what he expected. He then told me to go back up to the shop and figure out how to make my work look like that jewelry. I searched for books and articles, anything that would teach me what I wanted to learn. However, few could be found.

In our own small way, we hope to help change this situation with Bench Magazine. Here you will find articles from bench jewelers willing to share their abundant knowledge with you, and our own "Trade Secrets" section where you can learn tricks of the trade from other jewelers and share your tips with jewelers around the world.

Written BY Jewelers FOR Jewelers

All articles in BENCH magazine are written by working jewelers who are masters of their craft. So many articles in industry publications are written by professional writers, who don't have an understanding of jewelry repair or custom jewelry manufacturing. We have worked hard to bring you information from jewelers who not only possess excellent bench skills, but also possess the skill to put pen to paper (or fingers to keyboard) and explain in a clear, understandable manner the procedures they perform.

It is my prayer that you not only enjoy reading Bench Magazine, but that you will learn valuable information to increase your abilities, improve the quality of your work, and make your job easier and more enjoyable.

Brad Simon CMBJ, CMP
Publisher / Editor Bench Magazine
From Bench Magazine Volume 1 Issue 1, Summer 2001

Table of Contents

5   Introduction

The Industry

8   Is Retail Jewelry Truly a Recession Proof Business?
9   State of Affairs
11   Ultra-Customized Customer Service
13   Being Different
14   Creativity
17   Attitude IS Everything
19   The Master's Touch
20   Lessons from the Bench

Business Development

24   A Brief History of Business in America
27   3 Basic Business Principles
29   Business Entities
30   Business Plan
32   The Power of CAD Selling
34   Your Silent Partner

Employee Development

38   Dig for Gold
39   Managing Bench Jewelers
41   The Omission of Commissions
43   What Gets Rewarded Gets Repeated
44   Show Me the Money
47   What Jewelers Want
49   Boss, Manager, or Leader
51   Freelancing

Marketing

56   Creative Marketing for Creative Bench Jewelers
61   Selling Custom Design Jewelry Online
64   The 3 Magical M's of Marketing
70   Follow Your Customer's Lead - Text Them!

Table of Contents (con.)

Pricing
74 Value Based Pricing part 1
76 Value Based Pricing part 2
78 3 C's of Effective Pricing
83 Overcoming the BIGGEST Obstacle to Raising Prices

Shop Safety
86 A Pain In The Neck
88 Organizing the Messes
90 Workshop Safety Tips

97 Bench Magazine Series of Instructional Guidebooks
99 Additional Shop Management Books by Bench Media

Introduction

A story is told of two elderly gentlemen sitting on a porch one day rocking along in their rocking chairs. One of the men owned an old dog and he was lying on the porch alongside of his owner's rocking chair. The dog was whining and crying so much that finally the other man asked his friend what was wrong with his dog.

The dog's owner replied that the porch on the house was very old, and because of that there was a nail sticking up. This nail was sticking his dog in the side and was causing the dog pain, and that was why he was whining and crying.

"Why doesn't the dog move?" The friend asked.

"Well," the dog owner replied, "I guess it just doesn't hurt that much."

Now before you tell me that that was the stupidest story you ever heard, let me tell you about a similar story, and that is the story of Jewelry Stores all across America. The typical jewelry store has a great big nail sticking it in the side called a repair shop. This nail is bleeding the profits off most jewelry stores and their owners do little about it. They figure it doesn't hurt that bad to do something to correct it, and they reason that the repair shop is just a necessary evil of owning a jewelry store. They whine and complain about how bad it is, but just like that old dog they just lie there as the shop keeps bleeding the profits from the store and often causes the store to bleed to death.

The good news is that it doesn't have to be that way. With proper management the jewelry repair / custom design shop can be a major profit center for the average retail jewelry store.

The Industry

> **Quote Worth Re-Quoting**
>
> *"Make no little plans, they have no magic to stir men's blood and will not be realized. Make big plans; aim high in hope and work, remembering that a noble and logical plan never dies, but long after we are gone will be a living thing."*
>
> — *Lita Bane*

Is Retail Jewelry Truly a Recession Proof Business?

Brad Simon

I'll never forget the day back in the late 70's when my boss took me aside to talk. I was a bench jeweler for his downtown jewelry store, my first job out of college. I was married and we were expecting our first child. The economy was a mess and I was concerned how long I would have a job.

He told me not to worry because the retail jewelry industry was one of the most recession proof businesses to be in. When the economy is great – we sell jewelry, and when there is a downturn – we sell remounts and repairs. He said there were very few jewelry store closings during the Great Depression of the 30's (I've never checked that out, but he was old enough to have known). He reassured me that during an economic downturn the Bench Jeweler is the MOST important employee in a retail jewelry store.

Last week I was reminded of his little talk when I read some early statistics on jewelry sales for 2008. Every single category was down from 2007 except for one. Engagement and Wedding Rings, Platinum Jewelry, Diamonds, Colored Stones, Gold Jewelry, Silver Jewelry, Pearls were all down from last year. The one lone category that was not only up, it was up 16% over 2007 was Jewelry Repairs!

As you make plans for your Valentine's Day advertising and for the rest of 2009 Promote Your Shop Services! To be successful in 2009 you must keep your inventory levels low, train your staff to sell remounts and repairs, and provide your bench jeweler with continuing education so that they will be prepared to handle the increased workload.

Advertise Your Repair Services. Hold Re-Styling Events. Promote Custom Designed Remounts. 2009 will be the Year of the Bench Jeweler – Are you ready for it!

State of Affairs

Chuck Koehler

It's a brand new year. I think I'll take some time to give my opinion about the state of affairs regarding bench jewelers in an ever changing world.

A couple of months ago I started compiling the columns I've written through the years for another publication to be published as a book. Some of the old columns I hadn't read in years, but they brought back a lot of old memories and thoughts about how our industry has evolved over the last several years. The more I read, the more I began to see a pattern of where we've been (as bench jewelers) and where we're going.

We're very fortunate that we chose a career that doesn't have lower paid replacements coming into the industry. If you do good, honest work, you'll never be unemployed. The bench jeweler (just like the watchmaker) is becoming a dying trade and you should be proud that you do what you do. We 'make' the business run. Without us, the stores cannot sell their diamonds. Without us, the store can't sell the wedding bands to the customers getting married tomorrow that are just now buying their wedding rings.

Bench Jewelers have never been at the forefront of the business – until recently. Most people think of the person in the nice suit or dress with manicured nails when they think of their jeweler. They think of the person that waits on them across the counter as their jeweler. How many times have you had to explain what you do after you tell someone you are a 'bench jeweler'? People get a confused look on their face and ask you 'What is a bench jeweler?' I think that's about to change.

There are fewer and fewer bench jewelers in the trade every year, while there are more and more jewelry stores every year. Since most stores are in the business of selling the merchandise in their cases, the service aspect is simply a dreaded necessity. Most store managers will tell you they lose more money on their repair department than they make. This is especially true of the large corporate chains. They are driven by their stock price, not by the services they offer in each store. It's sad but true.

In reality, most customers are only concerned about price, not service as well. However, there will be more work for the decreasing amount of bench jewelers. But what I don't like about this trend is the lack of benefits and security that this presents.

The large chains are in a position to offer stock incentives, 401K's, medical and dental, and paid vacation to their sales staff. Most trade shops are only a couple of people working their butts off to keep up with the work. Vacation.......are you kidding? Who's going to cover the workload while you're gone? I don't have an answer for this, it's just an observation about where I think we're going.

Laser welding is a new technology that I personally have not signed on to yet. I know it's probably here to stay, but with my business, I can do without it *for now*. I am increasingly aware of the newer, cheaper models that are coming out all of the time. Someone told me to start watching E-Bay and they'll pop up there from time to time. Anyone that caught my breakfast speech in Atlanta last year knows that I'm all about knowing the basics, and then using the toys (aka...lasers) to speed up the process. Don't use the toys as your basis of skill.

Now, I have a slightly different opinion. As I'm seeing more and more laser welders entering the jewelry workshops, I'm seeing a whole new breed of skilled laborers using the machines. I can see how being proficient on a laser welder is not something everyone has a knack for. Some are better than others. Just like conventional soldering and stone setting. The laser welder is a complex machine that requires a very skilled person at the controls. I'm still a little wary of new jewelers entering the field and starting with the laser instead of the torch, but that's just the way this business is going so I'm trying to accept it.

Being a bench jeweler has about a ten to fifteen year learning curve. Education and experience is by far the best investment you can make in your career. There are many complicated procedures that we may do only two or three times a year. At that rate, it could take 10 years or more until you've done it enough to be good at it. The only way you can practice and learn those techniques is to spend years at the bench and to participate in Continuing Education.

Reading this magazine, attending our traveling road shows, and attending our annual conferences is a good way to advance your skill level. And quite frankly, the higher your skill level, the easier your life. Plus what I've found at our bench jeweler gatherings is that you get to meet other bench jewelers to talk shop with.

I remember when I was just getting started about 25 years ago. I spent the first part of my day screwing up the jobs on my bench. I then spent the rest of the day fixing what I broke that morning. As your skill level increases, so does your income. You are able to do the work much faster and you spend less time re-doing mistakes. Also, your frustration level decreases dramatically. I remember being so mad at a job I'd spent hours on, only to take it to my friend with 20 years' experience who would fix it in five minutes. Even though I was standing right over his shoulder watching him do the same thing I'd been trying to do, he did it perfectly the first time. When I would ask how he did it so effortlessly, he would just say he'd screwed it up so many times he finally figured out how to do it right. One consolation though, once you've figured out how to do something correctly, you'll do it that way every time. Then, that's one more skill you've got under your belt, and one less frustration in your life. It works that way. Believe me.

To wrap it up, be happy with your chosen profession. You go to work and work with precious materials every day. What you do affects people's lives in a very positive way. Most people go to work and hate their jobs. As a bench jeweler, no two days are ever alike because no two jobs are ever the same. Be proud of what you do and enjoy it … it's a good gig!

Ultra-Customized Customer Service

Brad Simon

Being a Bench Jeweler is more than a career, it's a passion; and it's also a profitable one in these days of customers who demand personalized service.

What a unique profession the bench jeweler is a part of. We have time honored techniques such as forging, sawing, filing, and many others that have changed little over the centuries, coupled with new cutting-edge technology such as laser welding and computer assisted design. These new technologies are already a part of several retail jewelry stores' shop. For many others they are just on the horizon.

For a jeweler to sit at a bench working on jewelry combining these diverse talents; regardless of whether they are repairing a customer's cherished treasure or creating a future heirloom, is more than a career – it is a passion.

I shall never forget the feelings I experienced the day I made my first piece of jewelry in a high school art class. There I sat, patiently sawing out a design from a brass cymbal the marching band had broken. As I sawed, the pendant evolved right before my eyes. Then, as I carefully polished the metal, it seemed to come alive – right there in my hands. What came alive was the passion within me to create jewelry. That passion has never ceased nor diminished to this day.

During the past few years, the jewelry shop has become more than just a passion; it has become a strong product category. It has become an important part of the retail jewelry store, and vital to the health of the jewelry industry.

The 1998 Jewelers of America Bench Jewelers Survey stated that stores with a jeweler on the premises averaged 20% of their sales volume from their shop. Also, the 1998 J.A. Cost of Doing Business Survey revealed that jewelry service from our shops is the third largest product category in our stores, exceeded only by diamond jewelry, and gold jewelry sales. Sales of shop services now exceed traditionally strong product categories such as color stone jewelry, watches, and pearl jewelry. It is a large, strong product category that continues to grow.

Over the past two decades, all successful retailers have placed more emphasis on customer service. For many jewelers, that meant better hours, nicer wrapping paper, or even a sales associate who remembered clients' birthdays. While all of these factors help improve a store's reputation for service, nothing can quite compare to a jeweler's ability to repair precious jewelry or set stones in a new mounting.

In the coming decade, customers will no longer want to be served only with broad gestures. They'll want service tailored to meet their specific needs. Those needs will range from the simplest repair to alterations in pieces you stock to complete design and fabrication services. In fact, I predict that the 2000s will come to be known as the decade of Ultra-Customized Customer Service.

When we provide our customers the services from an efficient shop, not only can we provide this customized service, but our store's image is enhanced as well. Customers begin to see us as professional jewelers, not just as some merchants peddling goods. They see us as someone who know what we are doing. They know we understand jewelry and can customize and make a piece of jewelry to meet their desires. When necessary, we can also repair their jewelry in an expert fashion. It does enhance our image, and we will not only get customers to come into our stores, but we will get those customers to come back into our stores again and again. The stores who provide ultra-customized customer service will be the ones who don't just survive in the future; but they will thrive!

Being Different

Martin Rugroden

More and more jewelers are designing unique pieces for their clientele. One reason is the custom jewelry market is more accessible through computer-aided designing (CAD) and computer aided manufacturing (CAM). Another more important reason is the customer's desire for more personalized jewelry.

In this age of mass merchandizing it is difficult to stand out when many chains or "box stores" are selling thousands of identical items like clothes, glasses, and cars. The jeweler who will take a few extra moments to suggest an additional gem or redesign to a customer in for a repair may enjoy a noticeable increase in income. Since the customer is already prepared to trust you with the repairs they will be more willing and open to entertain further suggestions to set themselves apart.

Colored gems are still a mystery to much of the buying public and unlike diamonds, they are not an easily quantified commodity. Because of the nearly infinite color variations, optical characteristics and the endless variety of shapes available today, it is less of a struggle for the jeweler to create a new, unique design using unusual gems.

Jewelers using one of the CAD programs find the process of designing, selling and building one of a kind jewelry less challenging than ever. The traditional methods of designing can also be used with great success for those wanting to distinguish themselves from the competition.

Using new and unusual gem designs will set a jeweler apart from the shop down the street. CAD programs can take an image of a gem and trace its outline with extreme dimensional accuracy. For those using traditional methods of designing, gently heating wax, or the gem and pressing them together will give an exact impression of not only the girdle outline of the gem but the depth as well. The picture shows an example of how striking designs can be accomplished using CAD. This can also be done using traditional methods as well.

If you are a traditional jeweler working with heat sensitive gems, or, any gem for that matter, you can quickly make a model by using a variety of casting methods. I use a watchmaker's watchcase filler called SPEEDI-FIT. Simply wrap the gem in a plastic wrap like Saranwrap and press it into enough filler to make an impression of the pavilion and girdle of the gem. Wait about 5 minutes for the SPEEDI-FIT to harden and remove the gem. Next, put a little Plaster of Paris in the cavity and let it harden. Now you have a model you can use to carve an exact setting for the gem. If you don't have the time to do this, ask your gem supplier to provide one for you. Now the danger of damaging the gem is lessened as well as possibly having to alter the finished piece to fit the gem.

By using new methods and out of the ordinary colored gems, your customer is less likely to shop for a lower price with your competitor. Instead of having to lower prices and lose profits to compete, the customer is very likely to stay with you.

Creativity

Brad Simon

Often, we think of creativity in the jewelry industry as it applies to designing jewelry, and although that is a necessary ingredient for a jewelry designer, I also believe creativity is what sets many master repair jewelers apart from the rest. When we at the bench are approached with a jewelry repair problem our creativity in problem solving is called upon, and how creative we are will often determine how successful we are in fixing the jewelry to our customer's satisfaction.

The following is a look at some of the deterrents to creative problem solving and some solutions to increasing our creativity.

Lost Item Syndrome

Have you ever noticed that you always find a lost item in the last place you looked? Well duh! If I found the item I was looking for why would I keep looking for it? Well that may work for looking for lost items, but that same philosophy is a major deterrent of problem solving. Often when we are faced with a problem to solve we take the same approach as finding a lost item and as soon as we find a solution that may work we stop looking for solutions to the problem. The trouble is the first solution we think of is seldom the BEST solution to the problem.

You have probably heard of the story of the truck that was stuck under a viaduct. A work crew had spent hours trying without success to pull the truck out from under the viaduct to no avail. A small boy walked up to one of the workers and asked what they were trying to do. The worker explained that the truck was too tall to fit under the viaduct and was wedged in tightly and they were trying to pull the truck out from under it. The boy asked why they don't just let the air out of the truck's tires! The workers let the air out of the tires which lowered the truck, and they drove it out from under the viaduct.

Was the young boy smarter than all the workers? Of course not. The workers just suffered from the Lost Item Syndrome. They thought of one solution that should work and was stuck trying that solution over and over with the same failed results. The boy who was not smarter or more creative just brought a fresh perspective to the problem.

How often are we like those workers? We think of a solution to repair a piece of jewelry and out comes the tools and the work starts with little thought as to whether this is the best solution or not. I cannot begin to tell you the number of times I have begun to fix a piece of jewelry only to find that what I started to do has resulted in a bigger problem to fix, and if I had only done something different to begin with the repair would have been much easier. And regrettably, with jewelry that realization often comes only after a stone has been chipped or the jewelry damaged further.

The solution to the Lost Item Syndrome is simply to never begin a project until we have thought of 3 to 5 different methods to fix the problem (I also suggest that the bigger the problem the more solutions you find). Then armed with multiple solutions you can evaluate them and determine the BEST solution from the beginning. The old adage that it is better to spend 1 hour in planning and 10 minutes in execution than spending 10 minutes in planning and 1 hour in execution, is so true.

Many people believe they are not very creative, however, often the problem is not that they are not creative it is just that they don't have the discipline to take the time to think of a variety of solutions. We all face time restraints and deadlines. We feel that if we take the time to think of different solutions we would need to stop working to do so. In order to overcome the Lost Item Syndrome, we need to stop thinking of time spent think of solutions as time spent not working. Any time spent thinking of ways to repair the jewelry in an easier, faster, or better method is just as much of your job as sitting at your bench filing, sawing or soldering.

Tunnel Vision Thinking

Once we begin to think of different solutions we often fall into the second problem what I call Tunnel Vision. Here we do think of different solution, however, our thoughts are narrowly focused around one solution and offer us little help in finding the best solution.

Recently I was installing a ceiling fan at my mother-in-law's house. I've installed many ceiling fans in the past and consider it a relatively simple task. The house is an older one and the electrical box in the ceiling from the existing light was not sturdy enough to handle the torque of the fan. The kit I purchased to install the ceiling fan came with two lag screws to fasten the new electrical box in the ceiling.

The problem I faced was that the wood in the ceiling joist was old and very hard, plus the 4-inch hole in the ceiling that I had to work through created a steep angle to the screws. Lag screws are heavy, thick screws. Under normal circumstances it would be difficult to screw them into the hard wood, and the steep angle made this nearly impossible. The first power driver I tried to use would not fit through the 4-inch opening. A short flexible shaft on the driver allowed me to get through the hole but the angle on the screws keep them from screwing into the wood. I tried using a socket wrench, and was able to hold the screws straight but the 4-inch opening did not allow me to swing the handle far enough to screw the screws in. I tried drilling pilot holes so that it would be easier to screw the lag screws into the hard wood on an angle, but the drill would not fit through the opening. After using an extension on the drill bit, I finally got the pilot holes drilled, but still could not screw the lag screws in. On and on the work went with numerous new solutions to my problem. However, each one ended with the same results.

After an hour of work my brother-in-law came in from a back-yard project he was working on and asked how it was going. I left out no details as I told him of all the problems I was having, to which he replied, "Why don't you just use wood screws instead of the lag screws?" Wood screws are thinner and sharper and had no trouble screwing into the hard wood on an angle. The electrical box was securely screwed to the ceiling joist and the ceiling fan was installed with no further trouble.

In attempting to install this ceiling fan I suffered from what I call Tunnel Vision Thinking. I had come up with numerous ideas to solve my problem, but my solutions were so narrowly focused I missed solving my real problem. My focus was on the lag screws and I saw my problem as getting them screwed in. Whereas my brother-in-law saw the real problem of securely fastening the electrical box in the ceiling. By not having the narrow focus on the lag screws he easily found a better solution.

Thinking Outside the Box is a phrase we are all tired of hearing; but is the solution to Tunnel Vision Thinking. When thinking of different solutions to the problems we face look to see if all the solutions have things in common. Do the ideas all fit neatly into a 'box' on 'tunnel'? If so think outside the box, get out of the tunnel; force yourself to come up with solutions that are completely different in your approach, and tools and materials used. Try to think of ideas that may seem ridiculous. Often it is after we think of ideas that at totally absurd and have no chance of solving our problems that we then think of the best solutions. It's not because the absurd ideas have any chance of working, it's because those ridiculous ideas gets us thinking in different directions, it gets us out of our box or tunnel and allows us to find the solution that will best fix our problems. And then again, sometimes those ideas that at first seemed so absurd, after giving more thought to them, end up being the best solution.

Attitude IS Everything

Dan Gendron

Most of us have had some exposure to concepts like those exposed by self-help gurus like Tony Robbins and the late Dr. Norman Vincent Peale, and for the most part, we can agree that those ideas and concepts are worthwhile. But how many of us actually use those principles in our role as repair department liaisons?

The truth is that whether or not we realize it, our attitude affects the results we experience in the repair department. It is no stretch to have a bright, happy attitude when we are selling what we enjoy, e.g. a large diamond, or something we have created. The real trick is to develop a happy, expectant attitude when it comes to repairs – especially watch repairs! I have many occasions to visit jewelers and I find more times than not; jewelers behave less than enthusiastically when they encounter a watch repair customer! As a matter of fact, most I observe, act as though the customer handed them a dead rat!

We need to realize that our customers are sensitive to the demeanor we show them in the sales interview. In a recent seminar I gave the analogy that when we act less than enthusiastic towards a watch repair customer, it is much like if a man went to an upscale women's clothing store and upon choosing an expensive dress for his wife the sale clerk says to the customer "Why would you want to spend that much money on that fat cow wife of yours?" But this is exactly what we are doing when we do not treat our customers' watches without consideration to the way *they* feel about them.

We in the jewelry trades tend to be very "jaded", that is, we see our customers items with the eyes of what *we* think is worthwhile. Just today, I received a call from one of my trade customers asking me if an Ingersol watch was valuable. He wanted to know this to make determination of whether or not his customers watch was worth fixing. This told me from the start that he had not perceived the real value to his customer, nor did he try to evaluate his customer's real feelings about the watch. We have no way of knowing what our customers really think about a watch unless we ask them!

In that vein, the last watch my father was wearing was Russian Chrono, not worth very much, but while he was in the hospital it was something he did not worry about losing. He died wearing it. I would not value that watch at its "actual value" – at least not to me. To me, it is so valuable that I will keep that watch running at least for the rest of my life and no amount of money could ever buy it!

Speaking of my Dad, the late Henri Gendron, the old gent had a way of determining the customer's feelings about their watch. He did this in a way from which we can all learn. When the customer handed him their watch he would say something to elicit a response from them, e.g. "What a nice watch. You must be proud of this!" or "They sure don't make watch like this anymore." Or some other platitude. Then he would listen to the customer's response to his statements. If they agreed (e.g., "Yes, I love this watch!" or, "My husband gave me this for our 20th wedding anniversary." Or some such), he got a confirmation from the customer that they were very interested in having their watch repaired. He then proceeded to give them a detailed estimate to repair the watch.

On the other hand if the customer said "Oh, this piece of junk?" or, "I never liked this watch." Or some such, he would immediately move over to the new watchcase and start selling them a watch. Your rewards will always match your attitude:

　　Poor Attitude, Poor Results
　　Good Attitude, Good Results
　　Excellent Attitude, Excellent Results

So the next time you see a repair customer, especially a watch repair customer, greet him or her with a smile. Then just watch and see. I think you will notice that watch repair customers aren't grumpy misanthropes like you thought!

The Master's Touch

Brad Simon

The difference between a Master Jeweler and an average jeweler is not so much learning advanced techniques but a mastery over the basic ones. For example, there is little difference between the soldering technique in the most complex hand fabricated item of jewelry and sizing a ring. What sets the Master's work apart is the meticulous execution of those techniques.

The downfall of many bench jewelers is not a lack of skills, but the determination and discipline to practice and fine-tune those skills to the degree of workmanship deserving the title of Master. Often what hinders our progress is not a lack of knowledge, but the apathy towards accomplishing our work that we have allowed to creep in. Over the years, it is easy to allow bad habits to develop; to hurry through our work or skip certain steps. To overcome this takes practice. Just like a sports player will practice before performing on the playing field, or a musician will practice before performing on stage, you need to continually practice before performing at the bench.

When was the last time that you did an actual practice exercise where you worked on a certain project just to develop a skill? Then critically examined the results to find areas that need improving and then practiced more to improve. (It is not practice that makes perfect, but perfect practice that makes perfect.)

Why not commit a little time each week, just to the development of your skills? Get back to the basics and practice those fundamental techniques that seem so simple and easy – those basic procedures that take only a few days to learn, but a lifetime to master. Remember, it is not the techniques that set the master apart. It is the meticulous execution of those techniques that does.

This is not to say knowledge and understanding of skills is unimportant. It is just that often all we seek is new knowledge to overcome a problem when what is needed at the bench is the development of the knowledge we already have.

Certainly, learning a helpful tip or a new trick can help anyone perform better work. However, unless and until the basic techniques are practiced and mastered can these new applications be performed with the perfection deserving Master Craftsman titleship. To accomplish this, spend less time trying to learn new tricks and spend more time mastering basic skills.

In addition to knowledge and understanding, one must also possess the God given ability to become a true Master. However, ability alone is not enough. Ability without the determination and discipline to develop it is only potential. Sadly, many a man and woman have gone to their grave with their potential still in them. In order to avoid this, one must practice to develop their skills to the best of their abilities. You see, practice does not make one a Master, but in order to become a Master one must practice.

Strive to accomplish the work of a master. This is a worthy goal of any jeweler regardless of where they are in the development of their career. Practice each technique and develop every skill with the standard in mind that this is the work of a true master. Even if this ultimate goal is never achieved (not everyone has the skills and abilities to become a Master Jeweler), the striving after it, the desire to become one, the reaching toward it, will create in you a better craftsman

Lessons from the Bench

Jurgen Maerz

It's been said that 90% of what you need to know to do a job is learned on the job. As Bench Jewelers we all know too well the truth of that statement. Anyone who has worked at a jeweler's bench for any length of time has learned a lesson or two from the School of Hard Knocks.

Here are a few of the lessons I've learned at the bench. Hopefully, many of you can learn from these lessons so that you don't have to repeat them. Or at least smile as you remember the time you were taught a similar lesson.

Tighten That One Prong Just a Little More

Making cluster Opal rings can be a challenge, especially the setting part. Four prongs, fragile Opals and little time. Amazing how we have the time to do things over, but do not seem to have the time to it right.

The ring was almost done, all the stones were set, all that was needed was to polish the prong tips and then buff the ring, clean it and deliver it.

So here I was at the polishing wheel when I realized that one prong seemed to be a little off the stone. Perhaps if I tighten it just ever so slightly, I can make it look better.

My inner voice told me to leave it alone, it has to be delivered and it looks just fine...

My perfectionist voice told me that I cannot let something like this get by and it is mandatory to fix it.

So what did I do? I went back to my bench, took Parrot beak pliers and ever so gently tightened the stone. Ok, this is better, but it needs just a wee bit more. And with that, I slipped and broke the opal.

The Diamond in the Watch Band

She was a good customer, who had come to our place of business many times for purchases, custom made things and repairs.

This time it was a simple little job: re-attach a safety chain on her diamond watch. The watch was made of platinum with little .02 ct diamonds in the case and on the band.

I re-attached the safety chain and noticed that the band was in need of cleaning. So I gently dipped it into our cleaning solution and then steamed the band. After I was done, I looked it over and discovered that a small diamond was missing from the band.

Oh oh.. It must have come out during steaming, I thought. So I looked for and found a small .02 ct diamond in my repair stone paper. It was an easy task to set it. I checked the rest of the band and the watch for loose stones and then proceeded to bring the watch to the front to be given to my boss. He handed it to her and when asked for the price he said that there was no charge.

She took the watch and commented on the clean band, and then surprised all of us by saying how generous we are as we had replaced her diamond as well ...

The Bridge

Working in a small jewelry shop can be a lot of fun. Some moments can be very unique and outright unbelievable. This happens to be such a moment.

A middle-aged woman came to my shop one day and asked if I do specialty repairs. I told her I can repair many things and wondered what it might be. She inquired if I can repair dental bridges.

Well, that depends on the kind of repair needed, I replied, I really would have to see it.

I understand, she said, reached in her mouth and pulled out a dental bridge and wanted to hand it to me for soldering. Needless to say that this was one repair I did not do.

Setting My Hair On Fire

Several years ago I was teaching a small jewelry class in my shop. I had five students and they were doing a project which included soldering. For this reason, several torches were lit to keep a small pilot light burning, so that they just needed to be picked up for soldering without needing to be lit every time.

I had just finished a casting, dowsing the flask in a bucket of water. As I turned around to take the flask from the bucket, I heard a noise that reminded me of the sound water would make if someone were to take a water hose and spray the garage door. At the same time, I felt something very hot on top of my head and heard several of my students screaming and pointing at my head. To my great dismay I realized that my hair was on fire.

In a split second, and without thinking, I stuck my head into the bucket of water, which I had just used to dowse the flask of the casting I just had made. As I came up from the bucket, the screams of my students turned into hysterical laughter, because the investment plaster made my face look like that of a mime: snow white.

At the time it was stylish to have a permanent wave type haircut. Well I burned it down to where it was about ¼ inch short, after my barber got through with me. So in 1980, I had a 2005 haircut.

I was very fortunate to have had a bucket of water nearby. When the hair of your head catches fire, it does not take too long to for major injury to occur. Always check your surroundings and be aware of any open flame. One ounce of prevention is better than a pound of cure.

The Chain Favor

One day a friend came to my shop and wanted me to replace a clasp on his golden Herring bone chain. He said he'd be back after lunch to pick it up. I accepted the job and removed the broken clasp and replaced it with a new one.

When I was done with it I realized that the chain was somewhat dull and thought I'd do him a favor and quickly polish it up a little. Well, having made jewelry for many years, I KNEW how to polish a chain. One wraps it around a wide felt wheel and then gently polishes small sections at a time.

Did I do that?
NO… I just held the chain in my hand, exposed a small section to the buff and polished away. Suddenly the chain was ripped out of my hand and began to rotate at very high speed around the spindle of my polishing motor, but not before slapping my hand repeatedly cutting me in several places.

I immediately turned off the motor and removed the chain from the spindle. It was completely ruined. A few band-aids covered the injury on my hand and $250 replaced the chain. What a costly favor this turned out to be. It could have cost me a finger or two as well.

Business Development

Quote Worth Re-Quoting

"Don't tell me you are too busy to plan. If you don't plan, you will be busy without accomplishing much and without realizing the fulfillment you need as a creative person."

- Lee Silber

A Brief History of Business in America

Brad Simon

Many people believe that in a Free-Enterprise economy you can get away with providing the least service possible at the highest price. But that only works in a monopoly – if there is no competition.

When businesses are allowed to compete with one another on a level playing field, providing the highest quality at a fair price always wins out.

Scottish Economist **Adam Smith** is considered the Father of Modern Political Economics. In 1776 he published his book **The Wealth of Nations**. It is a distinguished work of Enlightenment Scholarship; it advocated abolishing the special privileges and subsidies that benefited those well placed in British society.

Invisible Hand

In **The Wealth of Nations** Adam Smith described an Invisible Hand that would control markets. The Invisible Hand was the motivational power of ambition and self-interest in determining economic outcomes. This Invisible Hand would steer the economy to a most favorable outcome if only the government would get out of the way and let the markets do their work. If people believed they could get ahead by their own efforts, then they would, in their own self-interest, endeavor to do so. If enough people did this, markets that followed the principles of maximizing value through incentives would emerge.

Laissez-Faire

After Adams Smith's death in 1790 the French Revolutionaries adopted his economic principals and coined the phrase Laissez-Faire meaning a sort of utopian natural economic order that if left alone would develop into an optimally effective free-market system. A system where a government's obligation is to not interfere with the natural workings of markets.

American Business

Adam Smith's writings were directed to the British economic system of his day and spelled out issues that he thought England need to change for it to remain a world economic power. Smith never visited America, and never imagined his principles would be adopted there. However, many of America's founding Fathers read and were influenced by his writings. Men like George Washington, Ben Franklin, John Adams, Thomas Jefferson, Alexander Hamilton, John Jay, and James Madison used Smith's theories and ideas in forming the economic system of this new nation.

The democratic free-market system that they forged is the backbone to the Great American Entrepreneurial Spirit. President Thomas Jefferson in his first annual message to Congress stated: "Agriculture, manufacture, commerce, and navigation, the four pillars of our prosperity, are most thriving when left most free to individual enterprise."

Business in the United States

First Hundred Years

The majority of Business were privately owned and operated as Sole Proprietorships. These businesses operated under the democratic free-market system devised by our country's founders.

Around 1880

The Federal government assumed a stronger position in the private sector.

Monopolies began to spring up, and Large Corporations began to form.

After World War 1

For the first time Taxes started to take a significant bite out of profits. Between 1930 and 1950 the government's share of business profits grew to more than 20 percent of gross profits.

After World War 2

For the first time, borrowing became the accepted way to fund business expansion. Between 1950 and 1970 the cost of labor grew by more than 50% (the largest growth in history) and the government's share of profits increased to 40%. Between 1970 and 1980 Labor cost and cost to the government rose by another 10%.

Through countless regulations government made decisions for business and shared in its profits without doing any of the work. Government told farmers what they could grow, advertisers what they could sell, and schools what they could teach. Unwittingly, we had allowed a Fascist form of government to develop, with businesses privately owned, but centrally controlled.

To pay for all this, Business debt grew to a point where 60% of all American businesses would become un-profitable if interest rates grew to 15%.

1980 – 2000

During this time period, more wealth was created than during any other time in history. This favorable business climate was due in large part to substantial tax reductions in the early 80s, and large-scale government intervention in the economy was at as low a level as any American under seventy can remember. However, with tax increases during the 90's and a rise in government involvement brought this period to a screeching halt beginning with a slide in the stock market that began mid year in 2000 and lasted until the end of 2001.

The Business Climate Today

The business environment today is vastly different than what Adam Smith devised and what our founding fathers forged over two hundred years ago. Adam Smith outlined four roles of government as it relates to business and the markets.

The first is that government should not do anything that would affect the markets except to eliminate monopolies. Today many businesses enjoy special privileges from the government in the way of tax breaks, grants and bailouts. The government pays able body workers to stay home and pays farmers to not raise certain crops to keep the market price for them higher. The anti-trust case against Microsoft a few years ago shows an un-willingness of government today to break-up monopolies. This all creates an un-level playing field for business.

Second is that government is to provide an infrastructure for travel around and into and out of the country. In the past 25 years there has been a 250% increase in car and truck travel, yet our road and highways have only increased by 10% during this time. Our airports are understaffed and undersized. All this leads to congestion on our highways and airports that leads to delays in travel and shipping. This adds substantially to the cost of doing business.

The third role government should provide according to Adam Smith is a national banking system that is secure and sound. With the Savings and Loan scandal and ultimate collapse of a few years ago, the recent Enron fiasco and the instability of the dollar today, does anyone really believe the government is meeting this need of businesses?

The fourth role is to provide security for companies to conduct business in a safe environment. Burglaries and theft in the US are among the highest in the world adding millions of dollars to the cost of doing business. 911 provided Americans a tragic awakening to the fact that our national defense needed improvement and costed American businesses billions of dollars, not to mention the tragic loss of lives that day.

However, despite all of these short coming, the basic fabric of business today in America is still the free-market system devised by Adam Smith and implemented by our founding fathers. Any American can, at any time, decide to start and run a business without having to be born into a special class or family. Although the market is not completely free from government intervention it is still an open market for businesses to compete for the customers dollars.

In America today there is promise on every street corner and on opportunity up and down both sides of the street. For those who want to get ahead by their own efforts, America is still the land of opportunity, and success can be achieved through one's own efforts.

3 Basic Business Principles

Brad Simon

#1 The Customer is the BOSS

"You can get everything in life you want, if you just help enough other people get what they want" Zig Ziglar

To me that statement of Zig Ziglar is instrumental to business success. Everything in business success revolves around "other people" the customer. The term Free-Market could be defined as the customer is **free** to go anywhere in the **market** to spend their money. The key to business success then is getting the customer to want to do business with you.

To be successful in business takes three steps:

1. Find out What Your Customers Want.

This includes not only what products and services they want but also what price they are willing to pay for them.

2. Find a way to Provide it to Them.

This includes finding ways to provide what they want and at the price they are willing to pay.

3. Let Them Know you have What They Want.

If people do not know you have what they want, they cannot come to you to get it. You have to Market & Advertise your services and products.

Did you notice that all three of those steps centers on **Your Customers**?

Free Enterprise and Greed

Remember the movie **Wall Street** where Michael Douglas playing the part of Gordon Gekko stood up in front of the meeting of stockholders and proclaimed "Greed is Good! Greed is what drives business in America." Nothing is further from the truth. Remember, Hollywood is a land of fantasy and what comes from there in movies and television about business in America is often just that – **Fantasy**.

Business owners that are greedy and only thinking of themselves will find themselves soon out of business. Free-Enterprise businesses are all about the customers' needs and wants. It is a form of business that in order to be successful you MUST concern yourself with others.

2 Profits are the Life Blood of any Business

It's not how much you make that matters, it's how much you keep!

It is amazing to me how many people in America believe that a business can continue to lose money and still stay in business. Profits is not a bad word, there is nothing wrong with, nor shameful in making a profit. A business MUST make a profit to be able to continue to stay in business. Many people believe that when you start a business it is OK to have expenses greater than income because it is all Tax Deductible. However, that is NOT true. **A business must have a profit in order to survive.**

#3 Cash Flow Is King

You can make a profit in business and still go out of business, because of a lack of cash flow. You need to monitor the flow of cash coming into your business so that you will have cash on hand in time to pay the bills. Money is expensive to borrow, and interest rates can quickly absorb any profits a new business manages to make.

It is better to have no customers at all than to have customers who are slow to pay. If you do work for a customer and pay for all the materials and take your time to perform the work and then have to either borrow money to cover the time it takes the customer to pay, or at least, lose the value of that money while waiting for the customer to pay, that loss will erode the profits you made on doing the work. You end up spending your time to perform the work and have no profits to show for it. You would have been better off not spending the time to do the work.

If a trade account is behind in payments, I have no problem with holding their work I have in my safe, until they are paid up. If they don't like it and stop doing business with me, it is fine with me, because I'm better off not having a customer than having a customer who is continually slow to pay.

I tell them I have this special agreement with my bank. They don't do Jewelry Repairs and I don't Loan Companies Money!

Business Entities

Brad Simon

Choosing which business entity to use is an important decision; it can have important tax and legal ramifications. There are several fundamental structures that your business can take.

Sole Proprietorship

This is the easiest form of company to start and maintain. There is no formal business structure to set-up (although many states and cities require you to obtain a business license). Sole Proprietors have the least involved tax forms to file.

When you run your business as a Sole Proprietorship, you are the business. You, as the owner of that business, and your business are one in the same. This is the Main Disadvantage of Sole Proprietors. Your assets are the business assets and the business assets are your assets. (If your business is sued, they can take all your personal assets such as your home.) The same rule applies to liabilities. Your debts and the business debts are one and the same. The owner of a Sole Proprietorship is personally liable for business debts

During the first one hundred years of this country most businesses were privately owned sole proprietorships. Today many businesses start out as sole proprietorships and later change to another form of business structure because of favorable tax laws and to avoid the overwhelming increase of lawsuits.

Limited Liability Companies

This is the newest form of businesses in America and has become very popular. With an LLC owners have limited personal liability for business debts, however, they are easier to set-up and maintain than Corporations. States vary greatly in the regulation of LLCs and some states have high fees for them.

S Corporation

Owners of S Corporations have limited personal liability for business debts and from lawsuits. The corporation is a separate entity from the owners however it is not taxed; profits are passed on directly to the owner's personal tax returns.

The disadvantage of S Corporations is that they are more expensive to set-up and requires a great deal of extra paperwork.

C Corporation

C Corporations are a completely separate entity from the owners and offers the owners maximum protection from business debts and lawsuits. Tax laws are very lenient in Fringe Benefits paid to C Corporation owners.

Because C Corporations are a completely separate entity from its owners, the IRS taxes the profits of the corporation. Profits passed on to the owners are also taxed on the owners' personal tax return. Because of this, without proper planning, this double taxation can be very expensive. C Corporations also have the most paperwork to file and have the strictest laws to follow.

Changing Business Entities

You can change from one business entity to another at any time. However, once you change to a different entity type you cannot change again for 5 years. Before choosing which Business Entity you set up or change to you should consult with a Business Attorney and your Tax Accountant.

Business Plan

Marlene Richey

"If you want to reach your goal, you must 'see the reaching' in your own mind before you actually arrive at your goal." Said Zig Ziglar in "See You at The Top".

If you are driving from Newport, Oregon to Newport, Rhode Island, you will undoubtedly need a map. Otherwise, how would you know where you are going? And if you take a detour to Newport, Kentucky, you can find your way back because you have a map. A business plan is a business map.

It is a business principle that the chances of having a successful business grow exponentially if you have a written plan. It safeguards against costly mistakes. A business plan requires research, thinking, planning and writing. You get to look at your business from the top, the bottom and all sides. Jay Abraham, a marketing guru says: "You are surrounded by simple, obvious solutions that can dramatically increase your income, power, influence and success. The problem is, you just don't see them." A business plan helps you see them. Writing out your plan makes it possible for you to periodically go back to check your progress and see if you are on the right road.

A business plan is a constantly evolving work. It is a living document that allows you see where you want to go and where you have been. This is a tool you can give to potential investors, your spouse, banker, accountant, business advisor, and employees to show you are serious. The plan helps you identify potential roadblocks and obstacles that could hamper your success. It will not solve all of your problems, but what it will do is help you to see where changes are required. As situations change with your business or the business world, you can adjust your plan to reflect these shifts or the direction in which your business is heading.

If you go online you will find an overwhelming assortment of information about writing a business plan such as sample forms and the information you need to include. But there are basic concepts you should apply whether you run a corner grocery store or a bench jewelry company. A good business plan should have:

- who you are
- where you want to go
- how you plan to get there
- your immediate goals
- your ultimate goals
- the potential costs

It covers all areas of your business such as management, personnel, the market, your competition, your services, money and marketing. By putting it in writing you are creating a record of your choices.

The plan should not be longer than five pages for most small companies. Content is more important than size. Be as specific as possible in what you write. I recommend laying out your plan as an outline as it is easier to access information. Use bullet points. Your financial information should be accurate and realistic.

Here are the questions and information you need to provide in your business plan:

The Business

Is your company a sole proprietorship?

List a company background and overview of your services and a short history of the company.

List your general goals and projections for one and three years.

The Product

Describe your services in depth.

Who is your competition? What other bench jewelry companies have similar services?

Different services

What are your advantages and assets?

Where do you need improvement?

The Market

Who is going to use your services?

Where will you be located?

What are the advantages/disadvantages of this location?

Is it secure?

Marketing and Selling your Services

How are you going to reach your potential customer?

What types of media/technology will you be using?

Personnel

Include your resume/bio.

Who are the other people that might be a part of your business?

What are their qualifications?

What expertise or funding will they be contributing?

Financials:

Do you have the money to start and maintain your business?

How much do you need?

Include information that might have an impact on your business such as:

> A balance sheet shows your company's finances as of a specific date.

> Three years of projections. Use the formula:

Assets (what you own) – Liabilities (what you owe) = your company's value.

> An Income Statement on the other hand covers the activity in your business for a specific period of time and answers the question as to whether you are making money or not. This formula is:

Revenue (money coming in) – Costs (money going out) = Net Income.

Seek the advice of a professional if you need to.

Conclusions

Make it a short, concise statement.

Include letters of Recommendation or Credit References.

Follow these simple guidelines and you will be on the road to success. Having a business plan is a powerful tool to help you know where you are going and how to get there.

The Power of CAD Selling

Greg Stopka

As they say in the theological world, "necessity is the mother of invention" is just about how CAD or computer aided designing and I came together. I had several small jewelry repair service shops that were just getting by. Although I thought that I was pretty successful because of the number of shops under my belt, I was still struggling to pay the bills. About the time that I realized that I was either going to get out of the business or find another way, I went to Las Vegas for the jewelry convention. I decided to give it one more try and see if I could find something that would enlighten and motivate me – and boy did I find it.

I traveled to Vegas and started going through all of the booths one by one, stopping at only the ones that directly related to my business. There wasn't very many that connected but when I browsed through the miles and miles of jewelry product sameness I spotted something that made perfect sense. Jewelry designing by computer, what a brainstorm! What was obviously always in front of me never hit me on the head into thinking that I could sell design services with a computer. I always sold custom design with pen, paper and a creative mind, "what was so different with a computer", I thought. I strode up to the GemVision booth with great excitement and was sold that minute on implementing this technology into my business. My wife was not thrilled with the purchase but as always she was there for support and knew how much I needed a change in my life.

At that time I purchased two GemVision's Digital Goldsmith 2d designing programs on their statement of what the program could do. "Digital Goldsmith 2D Jewelry Design Software – Enhances communication between jeweler and customer by making it easy to perform custom design and remounts and allows your inventory to be expanded, interchanged and made more flexible right from your computer". That was enough for me to put down the required deposit.

After getting settled with the programs and training, I embarked on changing my stores to highlight Digital Goldsmith (DG) right in front of my customer. I set up a CAD sit-down area, overhead TV monitors that were connected to the designing computer and displayed colorful graphics that described what computer designing was all about. Within the first six months customers flocked to my new technology, my business soared 66%! Since I did not have physical inventory to sell because I was primarily offering repair services, CAD allowed me to communicate ideas onto a better canvas. Instead of doing pencil drawings or try to describe the design, which can lead to lots of miscommunication and frustration, I told the designing story through the power of computer designing. I sold better repair and better design because I could either bring up an inventory or camera scan in a customer's item, set different gemstones, matching wedding shadow bands or even set the stones into the metal to give my customer a finished look. My repair services became the driver for my custom designing. Customers came in for repair and I would suggestively sell an enhanced repair, a redesign, or a completely new design.

Selling jewelry doesn't just have to be limited to presenting out of a jewelry counter. The new opportunity in selling to your customer is in communicating your ideas in a creative, colorful and an emotional way. Customization and creativity will take precedence over physical selling. All things as we know it have a starting point and most are created through concepts and ideas. Selling with computers is the vehicle that turns you and your customer's ideas into reality. You can't put a price tag on that and it can never be shopped, negotiated, or copied by another because it comes from your ideas. The computer is the only way that jewelers can create with abandon because he or she can make mistakes with not having to think about the outcome. If the design isn't working then it can be easily deleted or erased and done over or manipulated.

The starting point for me was over six years ago when I fully embraced CAD. Now I have went further and implemented 3d computer designing (create 3d models that can be rendered lifelike and used to produce wax models for casting) with my 2d cut and paste programs. To this day I don't have physical inventory and still do quite well repairing and creating out of my three small studios. I have a saying when people ask me how I sell with nothing physical in my hand, I tell them that I have all the inventory I will ever need, it's all in my head waiting to be released onto my workable canvas.

Happy designing!

Your Silent Partner

Brad Simon

A silent partner is someone who is not actively involved in running a company but draws a percentage of the profits. Every person in the United States has a silent partner. It doesn't matter if you own a business or work for someone else, you have the same partner. This partner does not help in any way to make your business successful, yet it takes half of your profits!

Who is this partner of yours? It's the Government!

Taxes are the #1 expense of Americans Today. Income Taxes are made up of 3 or 4 different taxes.

- Federal Income Tax – up to 39%
- State Income Tax – up to 9.6%
- FICA (or self-employment tax) – 15.3%
- City or Local Taxes – up to 3%

The average American gives up between 42% and 55% of his or her income in the form of taxes.

"The single most important key to my success is a working knowledge of the tax code." **Bill Gates**

The Biggest Tax Myth

Tax Loopholes are for the Rich.
The truth is, Rich people don't take advantage of tax loopholes because they are rich. Rich people are rich because they took advantage of tax loopholes. Every single tax loophole that is available to rich people is available to ALL Americans. Only a fool will cheat on his taxes when there are so many legal loopholes available.

Arthur Godfrey, a popular humorist, once said, "I'm very proud to pay taxes as an American, but I could be just as proud to pay half as much." Many folks share that sentiment. Surely, no one objects to paying his or her fair share of taxes, but who wants to pay more than his or her fair share? Yet, many people unwittingly pay more than their fair share because of poor tax planning. Poor or no tax planning often results in loss of legitimate reductions of taxable income or loss of valuable tax credits.

Tax Avoidance VS Tax Evasion

Some people don't know the difference between tax avoidance and tax evasion. It's really very simple. The difference is about $10,000 and five years in jail. Tax Avoidance is taking all the maximum legal deductions to avoid overpaying your taxes. Tax Evasion is deliberately underreporting your income or evading to pay any taxes altogether. This is illegal and will get you into serious trouble with the government.

The classic description of tax avoidance was written by Judge Learned Hand in Helvering v. Gregory, 69 F. 2d 809, 810 (2nd Cir, 1934), aff'd 293 U.S. 465 (1935).

"Anyone may arrange their affairs to keep their taxes as low as possible. Nobody owes any public duty to pay more than the law demands."

In another famous quote regarding the U.S. income tax law, Judge Hand wrote: **"There are two tax systems in this country – one for the educated and one for the** uneducated." That is so important that it bears repeating. There are TWO tax systems in this country, and one is MUCH more favorable than the other.

If you're feeling guilty about reducing your taxes, then hear what Supreme Court Justice Sutherland had to say: **"The legal right of a taxpayer to decrease the amount of what otherwise would be his taxes, or altogether avoid them, by means which the law permits, cannot be doubted."**

Those who attempt to reduce their taxes may not always succeed, but those who don't, will not. Although there is no magic tax saving pill or strategy, there are many legitimate ways to legally and ethically reduce the income taxes you pay. By learning more about taxes, you will be able to lower your tax burden by taking legitimate tax breaks.

Justify All Deductions

Never buy something just because it is Tax Deductible. Even if you are getting a 50% deduction on your taxes **you still have to pay the other 50% out of your pocket**. Buy only what is essential for you to operate your business successfully and maximize all of your deductions, but never use the excuse that it's tax deductible to justify the expense.

Audit Proof Your Records

The reason it is so important to have the proper documentation is that without it, the deduction may not hold up under scrutiny. In other words, you could lose the deduction. When the IRS disallows a deduction, you are not only responsible to pay any tax that's due, you are also responsible for penalties and interest. And the penalties and interest are often more than the tax itself!

In the event of an audit, the burden of proof is on the taxpayer to justify the deductions. However, simply by keep proper documentations, you shift the burden of proof to the IRS to disprove the deduction. That really tips the scales in your favor!

Keep in mind that merely keeping the receipt is insufficient in the eyes of the IRS. You must also document what the business purpose of the expense is. Get into the habit of writing on the back of receipts what was the business purpose of the expense. It may seem obvious to you at the time what the business purpose is, but 3 or 4 years later when you are being audited it will not be as easy to remember. For any business-related meals or entertainment write on the back of the receipt who ate with you (even if the receipt is just for you), the business purpose of the meal or meeting, and what was the business-related subject discussed.

3 Types of Tax Accountants

The Go-Getter

They want to challenge the IRS on every ruling, they see every gray area in your favor and push the tax laws to the limit (and often beyond). If you come across this type of Tax Accountant don't walk away from them – RUN! The last thing your business needs is to be constantly defending IRS challenges in audits and courts. There are enough ligament deductions to take that you don't need the aggravation this type of tax accountant will cause you.

The Timid

This is the opposite of the Go-Getter. This tax accountant is afraid that anything out of the ordinary is going to set off a red flag and cause trouble with the IRS and as a result will not take ligament deductions for you. You may be paying their fee, but this accountant works more for the IRS than for you! Avoid this type of accountant as well.

The Middle of the Road

This tax accountant has a healthy fear of the IRS and will avoid Red Flags and Grey Areas on your tax return. However, they also know and believe that it is **Your Right to Pay the Legal Minimum Amount of Taxes.** They will take only Black & White deductions right out of the tax codes but will work hard for you to maximize all ligament deductions. Finding this type of tax accountant is well worth the effort.

Learn the Tax Rules Yourself

Having a good tax accountant is not enough. You need to learn the tax rules yourself. Remember what Bill Gates said? Learning the tax code was the single most important key to his success. The reason is simple. Even though you have a good tax accountant they cannot be with you every time you make a purchase to tell you whether or not it can be deducted from your taxes. They cannot be in every meeting you have to tell you what decisions you should make in your business to maximize your tax deductions. You have to know it yourself. Your accountant can only maximize your deductions from the information on the documents you bring them. You have to know how to prepare those document and what documents to bring to them.

The best tax advice I ever received was:

Know the Rules
Follow the Rules
Enjoy the Benefit of the Rules

Employee Development

Quote Worth Re-Quoting

"Leadership is the art of getting someone else to do something you want done because he wants to do it."

— Dwight D. Eisenhower

Dig for Gold

Brad Simon

Motivating people is similar to mining gold. In order to mine one ounce of gold you have to move tons of dirt, but you do not go looking for the dirt. You look for the gold. To motivate people, you must look for the good things they do (the gold). Anybody can find what is wrong. It takes a good leader to continually look for what is right, and give thoughtful, meaningful praise.

Pay Every Employee a Daily Complement

This forces you look for things to complement them on. At end of the day you have to find something to complement them on. It gets you to start looking for things early in the day. Once you get in the habit, you will find you are complementing your employees more than once a day.

We are always telling our jewelers things about their work that we want them to do better. When was the last time you told your jeweler things that they have done that you really like? When was the last time you showed your jeweler the things they did that you want them to repeat?

Abe Lincoln had a clipping from a newspaper in his pocket that he took out and read daily. It was by a writer who thought he was doing a great job as president and complemented him on the way he was handling the war effort. If he needed this daily reminder – how much more does your bench jewelers.

Make It A Habit

When a customer complements a job well done, the first thing that salesperson should do when the customer leaves the store is go back in the shop and pass the complement on to the jeweler. This should be done every time and before doing anything else (except maybe using the restroom). If there are other customers waiting in the show room tell them, "I'll be right with you I just need to finish up with the last customer". Then go back in the shop and say I just wanted to tell you that Mrs. Jones Said, "_____" then go wait on the next customer. It really does not take that long. The next customer does not have to wait long, BUT IT MAKES A HUGE DIFFERENCE TO THE BENCH JEWELER.

Managing Bench Jewelers

Brad Simon

After a recent seminar, a storeowner asked me what he could do to get his bench jeweler to come to work on time. He had tried everything he could think of (including nagging), but nothing seemed to work.

Now I know there are a lot of dependable, conscientious, highly motivated bench jewelers. However, as I travel the country putting on seminars on shop management, I find this to be a growing problem. Whether it is showing up on time or some other job function, more and more storeowners are asking how they can get their bench jewelers to do what they want done, and in the manner they want it done.

First of all, my advice is to sit down and talk with your jeweler. (Actually sit down and have a conversation not just make comments when he comes in late) Two things need to be accomplished in this conversation.

1 Find out why he comes in late.

It maybe lack of interest, lack of motivation, or lack of responsibility. However, it also maybe a legitimate reason, such as he needs to drop off kids at school or he shares a ride with his wife to work and cannot make it in sooner. If that is the case you can either adjust his work schedule or work out other arrangements for him to get to work.

2 You need to explain the importance of coming to work on time.

Often we expect things from our employees and have never fully explained what it is we want. Our Employees Can Not Do What We Want Done, If They Do Not Know What It Is We Want Them To Do!

You may find out that they do not come in on time because then they have to put jewelry out in the cases and they feel that is the salespeople's job. Knowing the reason they are habitually late will allow you to work out a solution. Maybe instead of putting out the jewelry, they can have other responsibilities, such as getting the shop ready (filling the steamer, etc.) or organizing the shop's work and filing the work-in-progress slips. Something that needs to be done and they feel is related to their job in the shop.

Don't assume they just lack the motivation to come to work on time. It maybe any number of other reasons. Talk with them to find out the reason, then you will be in a position to find a solution you both can live with.

If it comes down to lack of motivation, that they are just not interested in coming on time. You have your work cut out for you. But don't despair, there are thing you can do to help the situation.

First of all understand that you CAN NOT motivate him. No one can motivate anyone but themselves. You have all heard the statement; You can lead a horse to water, but you cannot make it drink. Well, I've coined a new phrase; You Can Lead A Jeweler To A Bench, But You Can Not Make Them Work. The desire to work is just like the desire to drink. It must come from within the individual. You cannot force anyone to work anymore than you can force them to drink a glass of water.

Now, a long time ago, farmers learned that they can get their livestock to drink adequate water, if they feed them enough salt. By adding salt to their diet the livestock becomes thirsty and will want to drink.

In business it is no different. We need to find something to "feed" our employees to get them to want to work.

Dwight Eisenhower said, *"The key to leadership is to get people to do what WE want done, because THEY want to do it."*

This "something to feed them" falls into two categories:
- **Negative Consequences**
- **Positive Reinforcement**

Negative Consequences is common in disciplining children. If they misbehave, they get a spanking, etc. Although not talked about as much, it is also effective in changing behavior in adults. It is what the police use to get motorist to obey the speed limit. If you break the speed limit, you will receive a ticket.

In business, you can do something similar. If an employee continues an undesirable behavior, such as coming in late, they will receive a negative consequence. These can range from reprimands, loss of pay, suspensions, and ultimately firings.

If your jeweler works on commissions, you may find that you are returning work to the shop to be touched-up or stones tightened. This is because they are rushing through the job to get more finished. A solution maybe to dock 10% from the commission paid on all returned work. Or if jobs come out of the shop late pay full commission on work 1 day before due date, 80% commission if finished on due date, and 50% commission on work done after due date. Plus, no commissions paid until past due work is finished.

Although this can be effective in changing behavior, you need to be careful not to rely on these too often. You do not want to create a "firings will continue until the moral improves" atmosphere. Often the better approach is to provide positive reinforcement by providing a reward when the desired behavior is received rather than punishing the undesired behavior. Putting your jewelers on commission is a form of positive reinforcement. When your jewelers perform their work to your standards (desired behavior), they are paid (reward).

However, commissions are far from the only means of providing positive reinforcement. There are many ways to provide incentives and they do not necessarily have to be monetary rewards either. I heard of one lady whose husband had a very well-paying job. Money did not motivate her to perform at her job. However, her employer saw that she liked to give her opinion on how the store should be run. So, he told her if she meets certain weekly goals, he would give her 15 minutes of his undivided attention, and she could express her ideas. She never missed a week.

For other ideas see the book "1001 Way To Reward Employees" by Bob Nelson. (You can get it at your library or any bookstore) Be creative and find what incentives you can provide that your employees desire (if they do not desire it, they will not be motivated to receive it)

Both negative consequences and positive reinforcement can be used together effectively. For example, if the jeweler shows up on time every morning for a month, he will receive an incentive. If he receives the incentive three months in a row, a larger reward will be given. However, if he is late five or more mornings during a month, he will receive a warning. Three warnings in a 6-month period maybe ground for dismissal.

The fun thing about managing is there is no ONE right way to do things, and what works today may not work tomorrow because things change! Have fun, be creative and most important of all sit down and talk with your jewelers. Find out their likes and dislikes. **Remember: You Need To Work Together As A Team – Not As Adversaries**

The Omission of Commissions

Brad Simon

Commissions, A Reward for Doing Work Fast & Sloppy or An Incentive to Perform More Work

Putting jewelers on commission can have its benefits, and many jewelry stores have found it advantageous to do so. However, doing so may create problems for many stores.

First, it puts all the responsibility of increasing productivity on the jeweler. Granted, there are those jewelers who need this motivation to get work done in a reasonable amount of time. However, there are many issues that influence productivity that are beyond the control of most bench jewelers. These include take-in procedures, shop design, job information control, interruptions, lack of equipment, work conditions, etc.

The front-end of many stores are so disorganized that it is impossible to run a productive shop. For management to put their jeweler on commission in these circumstances is irresponsible.

In addition, many jewelers do not know how to be productive. They are not taught in school how to schedule jobs and organize work to be more productive. To put them on commission and make it their problem without providing training is also irresponsible.

Before management puts any jeweler on commission, they need to take a long hard look at these issues and make necessary changes. You need a store with the front-end set up efficiently before you can expect jewelers to function under a commission system.

The second problem is pricing. Many stores have their prices on repairs set far too low. They lose money on repairs and make-up for it through sales of new merchandise. Putting jewelers on commissions in these circumstances is totally irresponsible of management. If the price you charge is too low – then the commissions you pay would also be too low, and your jeweler would have no method to make-up for it as you do with sales. Before putting your jewelers on commission make certain your prices are set correctly for your store. Do Not Just Copy Someone Else's Prices. Do the work and make certain your prices are right for your area.

The third problem with jewelers on commission is it only motivates the jeweler to produce more work. However, most stores want more from their jewelers. In addition to quantity, they want quality, they want jobs finished on time (when promised), they want a team player, they want a jeweler to come to work on time, etc. A jeweler on commission will have the natural tendency to do the work that pays more and not do or procrastinate on the others.

In addition, just because work is up in the shop does not mean profits are. For example, a jeweler may solder a crown and set a stone, but in his haste he melts three crowns. The job may be done quickly, the shop's output increases, and the jeweler's commissions are up, but profits are down. Or it may be quicker to use too large a piece of gold stock to size a ring up and then file down (a waste of inventory) then to roll out the correct size gold stock. The work gets done quickly but profits are down because of it.

An incentive program such as paying commissions is not a one size fits all. It may or may not work for you. Just like there are different ways to re-tip a prong, set a stone, or size a ring, there are different methods to run a shop and motivate a jeweler.

Tying performance together with compensation is a good method of motivation. Just be certain you know what performance is being compensated.

What Gets Rewarded Gets Repeated

Brad Simon

A story is told about Don Drysdale the famous pitcher for the Los Angeles Dodgers. One year the Dodgers offered Mr. Drysdale a bonus if he kept the amount of walks under a certain number for the year. Management desired to keep the number of opponent base runners to a minimum. It seemed like a good idea to offer a bonus on limiting the number of free passes to first base.

As the story goes, on occasion when he had a three ball no strike count, facing the fact that one more ball and the batter would walk hurting his chances of receiving the bonus, he would throw AT the batter. If he hit the batter, they would reach first base on a hit batter charge, not a walk. A hit batsman did not count in his contract, only walks.

Don Drysdale received his bonus that year, and the Dodgers learned to be more careful in establishing what they want to accomplish in setting their bonuses.

Many retail jewelers have felt the same disappointment as the Dodger management. Wanting to generate more work out of their shop, they put their jewelers on commission or other incentive program. However, what they found is the quality of work dropped as the jeweler hurried to finish more work. In addition, large time-consuming jobs lay around the shop unfinished as quicker jobs are finished earning the jeweler more money.

A problem arises when management says one thing but rewards something else. For example: you can preach till you are blue in the face about quality but if you only reward quantity then speed is what you are going to get. For example: A jeweler may hurry through 10 jobs performing mediocre work and receive only one or two back because of not reaching standards. He can re-do those two jobs in less time than it would take to slow down and do all ten jobs correctly.

Or a jeweler sizes a ring, checks all the stones, and tightens the loose ones, as you would expect him to do. However, if you only reward speed (by paying commissions) then it would be faster for him (and more profitable) to size the ring and turn it in. When you check it and find loose stones and return it to him, he tightens them. He spends no more time sizing the ring or tightening the stones. However, he saves a lot of time by not checking the stones on all the rings he sized.

If you want both (quantity and quality) you need to reward both. If you try to gain both by rewarding one and punishing the other when not received (making them do it over without pay) you will not get the second item if they think the added reward outweighs the punishment. You are only fooling yourself if you think you will get something just because you ask for it yet reward something else (ask for quality but reward speed regardless of quality). To run an efficient shop, you must be consistent with what you say you want, and what you reward.

Show Me the Money

Brad Simon

Show Me the Money! Cuba Gooding Jr. demanded in his Oscar winning performance in the movie Jerry McGuire. Quickly that line became the battle cry of workers all across the country. Show me the money, they asked of their employers. Show me the money, and I'll improve my performance. Money, after all, is the greatest reward, and the greatest motivator – or is it? Cuba Gooding Jr. played the part of Rod Tidwell, a football player desiring and demanding the multi-million dollar contract the other star players were receiving. Each year I watch these multi-million dollar athletes compete, and wonder; If money is such a great motivator, why do so many of today's players seem LESS motivated to perform on the playing field than many of the "Under-Paid" athletes of the days of my childhood?

This past fall I had the opportunity to speak with two employees from different companies, just after they received their "Annual Employee Review" from their employer. These employees received vastly different reviews; however, both were equally outraged at their bosses.

The first employee told me she could not believe the review she had received. Her boss had nothing good to say about her. She worked hard all year to get the work out on time, but that wasn't enough. She worked to improve her skills, but he wanted her to do better. She tried to improve the store by doing more and more for the store, but he wasn't satisfied. Nothing she had done seemed to please him and she was heart broke.

I expressed my empathy for her situation and said, "to top it all off, you were probably expecting a raise with all that hard work weren't you."

"Oh, I got a raise," she said. "Quite a large one and an increase in my Christmas Bonus."

"Well then, doesn't that show you how much he appreciates your hard work," I responded.

"If he appreciates me so much, he should have told me," she exclaimed. "If he doesn't value all my hard work, I'll show him. I'm not going to knock myself out around here anymore."

The second employee gave me quite a different story. She told me how her boss had expressed his gratitude for her work. He told her how valuable she was to the store. The awards she won and the accomplishments she achieved had brought new customers to the store, and how lucky he was to have her work for him.

"That's great," I said, "I bet you're going to try even harder next year, aren't you?"

"You got to be kidding," she shot back. "I didn't receive a raise! If he doesn't pay me some of that extra money I made for him, I'll show him. I'm not going to try nearly as hard next year."

What is an employer to do? Both of these employers had valued employees. Both showed their appreciation, one through a pay increase and one though sincere praise. However, both employees were upset and vowed to quit working so hard.

To find an answer I turned to numerous management books and found Frederick Herzberg. He is considered the father of job enrichment and one of the major management philosophers of the twentieth century. Through his studies of management thoughts, he divided work issues into two categories: Dissatisfiers and Motivators.

Dissatisfiers are the primary cause of dissatisfaction and de-motivation on the job. Motivators are the primary cause for satisfaction and motivation on the job.

Dissatisfiers include:
- Salaries
- Interpersonal relationships
- Work conditions
- Company Policy
- Supervision
- Security

Motivators include:
- Achievement
- Recognition
- Interesting Work
- Challenging Work
- Responsibility
- Growth

Dissatisfiers will not motivate workers. Although you can achieve satisfaction in these areas, satisfaction does not increase motivation. However, when any of these areas fall below the level that an employee feels is acceptable, dissatisfaction will occur.

For example, if poor working conditions exist workers may become dissatisfied and unmotivated to work. By improving conditions moral will improve and workers will no longer be dissatisfied. However, a level of satisfaction is all you can achieve with working conditions. You cannot continually improve conditions beyond this level to create an environment to motivate workers to excel.

These levels of satisfaction are subject to change over time. They are dependent on the laws of diminishing return. For example, a salary level that is acceptable today may not be satisfactory five years from now.

Motivators are the primary cause for worker motivation. They are the stimulus for job enrichment. They provide opportunities for challenge and growth and develop the desire to excel and achieve.

According to Herzberg, achievement is the single strongest motivator. Achievements motivate a person to go on and try to accomplish a little bit more. This achievement can be accomplishing something for the first time or doing something better than ever done before.

The second strongest motivator is recognition. This occurs when a person achieves something and someone else recognizes that accomplishment in some way.

The job situations of the two employees I spoke about is a classic example of the Herzberg Theory of Dissatisfiers / Motivators. The boss of the first lady made the mistake many managers make. Thinking they can motivate their employees solely through the area of dissatisfiers, namely money. This, at best, creates contented workers not motivated ones. By itself, this will create satisfied workers producing adequate, mediocre work. In the particular situation given above, the employee was paid a salary that in her estimation was more than adequate. Offering her more money did not (and could not) motivate her to higher levels of performance.

The second boss realized that offering sincere praise for accomplishments provides a strong stimulus for motivation. However, the employee's perception of lack of pay dissatisfied her to the point that nothing could motivate her until the salary level was increased.

A compensation method that has gained popularity in recent years is to place bench jewelers on commissions in order to help motivate jewelers to improve productivity. This can be an effective method of compensation provided it is not seen as the only method use to stimulate motivation.

Over the past couple of years, I have observed a trend developing. That is during the first year or two bench jewelers placed on commissions work harder and their pay level increases. Then, after this initial period the pay begins to level off.

Herzberg's Theory explains this phenomenon. Bench jewelers are typically under-paid. Given the opportunity to increase their pay, they work harder to raise their pay. However, once they have achieved a satisfactory pay level their desire stops, until they become dissatisfied with the new pay level. With constant reminders from the industry (and from many of their bosses) that they are now paid above average; dissatisfaction with this new pay level is highly un-likely.

So, what's an employer to do when they have a valued employee? First and foremost, make certain they are not un-motivated from lack of pay. If they feel they are under-paid for their efforts nothing else you say or do can motivate them. Next, provide an enticement that will motivate them and keep them motivated by offering more opportunities for achievement, and then give recognition when that achievement occurs. Show Them The Money AND THE PRAISE!

What Jewelers Want

Brad Simon

Recently I heard an interesting story about the building of the Golden Gate Bridge. During the initial building of the bridge no safety devices were used and many of the workers feared they may fall to their deaths. However, during the last part of the project, the construction company stretched a large safety net under the bridge at a cost of $100,000. At least 10 men fell into it and their lives were spared.

What is interesting is that 25 percent more work was accomplished each day, after the men were assured of their safety. That increase in productivity more than paid for the safety net, not to mention the value of the men's lives that were saved.

When management provided the workers what THEY wanted, a safe, secure workplace; management received what it wanted, increased productivity. The result was the bridge was completed under budget and ahead of schedule. No monetary incentives could have accomplished so much.

One of the difficulties of managing lies in knowing what your employees want. An interesting study was done a number of years ago at General Electric's Hawthorn Plant. Management and employees were given a list of ten items. They were to list the ten items in order of importance to employees. The results are quite enlightening.

Management's list of what employees most wanted from the company they worked for was as follows:

1. Good wages
2. Job security
3. Promotion and growth within the company
4. Good working conditions
5. Work that keeps you interested
6. Personal loyalty to workers
7. Tactful disciplining
8. Full appreciation of work done
9. Sympathetic help on personal problems
10. Feeling in on things

However, when the employee's lists were compiled the results were much different. Their list was as follows:

1. Full appreciation of work done
2. Feeling in on things
3. Sympathetic help on personal problems
4. Job security
5. Good wages
6. Work that keeps you interested
7. Promotion and growth within the company
8. Personal loyalty to workers
9. Good working conditions
10. Tactful disciplining

What is interesting about this study is not only that management and employees differed in their responses, but also in how the two list compare. The three items that management listed as the top three, the employees listed as 4, 5 and 7. Fairly important, middle of the road issues, but certainly not the most important. However, the three items employees listed as 1, 2, & 3. Management listed as 8, 9, and 10! What employees most wanted from their company, management was least likely to give it.

Although the Hawthorne Study and the building of the Golden Gate Bridge took place during past generations, today's management can learn much from them. Our employees may or may not want the same things as these employees wanted. What's important for us to understand is that they may want different things than what we think they want. When we determine what it is they really want and provide it as an incentive, then our shops will become more productive, and our employees will be happier and motivated to excel.

Boss, Manager, or Leader

Brad Simon

The titles Boss, Manager, and Leader are often used interchangeable and seen by many as meaning the same thing. But are they?

Bosses

When I think of great Bosses of history I come up with a short list. The most famous Boss in America is most likely Al Capone of Chicago. Then of course you would need to add to the list Carlo Gambino of New York. And Bugsy Siegel of Las Vegas would make the list. There are other names you could add, but this is not a list of names you would want to be remembered being associated with.

Bosses have a plan for their organization and know what needs to be done to accomplish it. Their job, as they see it, is to let everybody know what to do and how to do it. They know what is necessary to be successful and all they need is for their people to follow their orders.

Bosses are often seen like playground bullies playing 'King of the Hill'. They tend to be domineering, demanding and want everything their way. Bosses Boss People!

Managers

I've tried to think of well-known Managers and could not think of any to compile my list. Even Google was no help. A search for 'Famous World Managers' came up empty. Google gave me a list of famous Baseball Managers (for some odd reason baseball calls their Head Coach a Manager), and then goes on to list famous Leaders mistakenly thinking they are managers.

Despite this, the fact is Great Managers are needed for any business to be successful. Managers are wonderful at organization and systemization.

Think of a warehouse full of supplies. Managers are needed to organize and oversee all those items. The supplies are arranged neatly on shelves in logical order. When supplies are low, new ones are ordered and placed in their slot on the shelf. Managers have and are devoted to their systems and procedures.

Great Managers and management skills are needed to control business finances, raw materials, inventory, supplies, scrap metals, tools and equipment.

People, however, don't want to be managed and will resist if you try. A long time ago I heard the saying 'You Manage Things but you Lead People'.

Managers try to control everyone and, just like those supplies in the warehouse, plug people into their plans. Managers put their systems and procedures ahead of all else and see their people as just another item to be use for the betterment of the organization. Managers Manage People!

Leaders

To compile a list of Famous World Leaders is an endless task. From Business Leaders to Military Leaders, Political Leaders to Religious Leaders, history is full of Great Leaders. Leaders Create and Make History!

Sam Walton became the richest man in America and was one of the great business leaders of the past generation. Regardless of what you may think of what Walmart stores have become today long after his death, his values and philosophies on business are timeless virtues.

In his autobiography *Made In America* Sam Walton wrote; *"What's really worried me over the years is not our stock price, but that our managers might fail to motivate and take care of our associates. I also was worried that we might lose the team concept or fail to keep the family concept viable and realistic and meaningful to our folks as we grow."*

Did you catch the difference? Bosses and managers tend to focus on themselves and their plans for the organization. Leaders focus on their people. Certainly, leaders have systems and policies concerning their employees, but they are a distant second to caring for their people. When systems and procedures are placed ahead of people you will end up with a system and no people to work it.

Leaders have a vision and plans for their organization, but they focus on the abilities and talents of their people and how they can help them develop those abilities and talents to fulfill those plans. Leaders listen to the dreams and aspirations of their people and seek ways to accomplish the organization's plans though achieving the individual's goals.

Leaders provide a vision for the organization and then inspire people to want to be part of that vision. They challenge and encourage people to develop and improve themselves and thereby creating a better organization. Leaders Lead People!

Bosses are Dictatorial, Managers are Manipulative, but Leaders are Inspiring. **Which one are you?**

Over 3,000 years ago King David ruled Israel and was loved and admired by all who lived there. The book of second Samuel records this testimony of his: *These are the last words of David: "The one who rules the people with justice, who rules in the fear of God, is like the morning light when the sun rises on a cloudless morning, the glisten of rain on sprouting grass."*

What a challenge for us – that our leadership would be as encouraging to those we lead as the first rays of sunlight breaking through the dark of night and be as refreshing to them as a morning shower on the blades of grass.

Freelancing

Brad Simon

Contract Work, Lease Department, Independent Contractor, call it whatever you want, it still amounts to the same thing. And that is your jeweler leaves your employment and sets up their own independent business to do the same work they were doing as an employee. In multi-jeweler shops you can set-up your key jewelers as Independent Contractors while keeping other on as employees or you can set-up you whole shop with each jeweler operating their own business.

Advantages for Store
- Keeps Good Employees
- Reduces Taxes & Benefits
- Reduces Overhead
- Stabilize Cost

Over the past couple of years, I've seen a new trend developing. Recently I've been receiving more and more phone calls from storeowners looking for experienced bench jewelers stating that they are having more trouble than ever before trying to find qualified jewelers to work for them. Over that same period, I've also heard from more and more bench jewelers stating that they have now started their own business.

One way to keep a good bench jeweler from leaving your store to set-up their own business is to offer to allow them to work as an Independent Contractor at your store. You get to keep the services of an experienced jeweler whose work you like, and they get to start their own business. **It's a win / win situation for all involved.**

In addition, you no longer have to pay Social Security and Medicare, Unemployment, or Workers Compensation taxes on their salaries, or pay for any employee benefits for them.

Your stores overhead is reduced as all shop expenses are now the responsibility of the jewelers, not yours. Plus, a major benefit to the store is your cost on jewelry repairs is stabilized. You will know from the price list your jeweler provides what each repair will cost you BEFORE the job is ever started. No more inflated labor cost because the jeweler took longer than expected. No more paying for a second crown because one melted or for lost or chipped stones!

Advantages for Jeweler
- Controls Future
- Owns Own Business
- Tax Advantages
- Established Account

The major advantage for the jeweler is you now control your own future. You own your own business and can set your own prices. You can decide how much you want to work and whether or not you take on other customers in your spare time to build your business. Your hours can be more flexible, because, as an independent contractor you set your own hours. However, keep in mind you must still satisfy your customer's needs (i.e. your former boss) – so you must agree on a work schedule.

Another major advantage working as an Independent Contractor for a store is that you get to start your business with one major account. Being able to start a new business knowing you already have a constant stream of work coming in is a huge advantage to anyone starting a new business.

In addition, you can now take advantage of all the tax benefits of owning a business.

Disadvantages for Store
- Less Control Over Work
- Responsible if Misclassified

Because your jeweler is no longer your employee you have less control over their work. However, this does NOT mean that you cannot set quality standards and return any work to be redone for not meeting those standards. You can also set promise dates and require that the work be finished and returned to you by that date, as well as asking for the occasional job done while the customer waits. And you can also set a schedule of hours of the day and days of the week that they need to be in the shop for you to use their services. In this respect your relationship with your jeweler's new business is no different than any shopping mall that requires stores to be open during certain hours and days of the week.

If the IRS or any number of other federal or state agencies audits your business and reclassifies your jeweler to an employee of yours and not an Independent Contractor, you will be responsible for all back taxes and fines. Because of this it is important that before you enter into an Independent Contractor Agreement you learn all about employee classifications and that your jeweler is complying with all of them. It's not hard to meet the qualifications and the documents can easily be found on the Internet or your tax accountant. However, if your jeweler does not meet the qualifications YOU will be held responsible – so make certain you have all the needed decimations BEFORE you start in the agreement.

Disadvantages for Jeweler
- No Guaranteed Salary
- Pay Business Taxes & Fees
- Business Insurance

One of the biggest disadvantages for the jeweler is you no longer have a guaranteed salary coming in each week. You will need to live on the profits you generate from your new business. For many this takes a while getting used to.

Another major disadvantage is you no longer have taxes withheld from your paycheck and you have to file quarterly payments to the IRS. The amount of money you will owe is quite a shock to many first-time business owners. However, the plus side is since you own your own business there are many tax deductions that are now available to you that you could not take as an employee.

In addition to business related taxes you will also have to pay any license fee or any other business fees required by your state or city. You will also have to get business insurance and pay for all your tools and supplies and any other expense related to your new business. Be sure to plan for all these expenses and include their cost into the prices you set of your services.

Items to Consider
- Rent
- Shop Equipment
- Work Schedule
- Payment of Invoices

In many stores with Independent Contractors the store provides the space for the shop to the jeweler for free. In return the jeweler gives first priority to the stores work above any other work the jeweler may take in. In addition, the store can advertise they have a jeweler on the premises, and when needed the jeweler provides while you wait services for the store. This is generally a good agreement and does not violate any of the 'tests' that the IRS and other government agencies have for determining the classification of the worker.

In addition to the rent the store may also own and supply certain shop equipment such as ultrasonic and steam cleaners, and polishing equipment. With the store owning this equipment there is no problems created when sales personnel need to use it to clean and polish jewelry for a customer. In exchange for using the store's equipment the jeweler maintains and services the equipment for the store.

A work schedule should be worked out in advanced. Although the jeweler is now an independent business and has the right to set their own hours of operation the store is still dependent on their services to meet their needs during their business hours. A general schedule needs to be mutually agreed upon and maintained for the smooth operation of both of the businesses involved.

A payment schedule also needs to be discussed and agreed upon. Just because the shop is provided free rent does not mean that the jeweler doesn't have other expenses to meet and also needs to be able to provide for his family. Payment of all invoices needs to be made in a timely manner on an agreed upon schedule. If not met the jeweler has the right to refuse delivering any more finished jobs until the past due amounts are paid in full.

There are other issues that may arise during the course of business. However, if both parties involved works together for a solution that benefits both companies, this type of business arrangement can truly be a Win – Win situation for all involved.

Marketing

Quote Worth Re-Quoting

"The aim of marketing is to know and understand the customer so well the product or service fits him and sells itself."

- Peter F. Drucker

Creative Marketing for Creative Bench Jewelers

Marlene Richey

It doesn't matter if you are a bench jeweler, a gemologist, a jewelry designer, or a consultant in the jewelry industry, there are things you can do to ensure your business gets noticed and grows. Whether you work out of your basement, own a store, or work for someone else, you possess specialized skills that are highly marketable. And, whether you are thinking about starting a business or not, you can always improve your visibility. As these articles will show, there are some basic as well as creative things you can do to ensure you start generating interest in both your services and products.

Many of my suggestions are geared towards owning your own business or having a repair shop, but it doesn't mean that if you aren't in this category you can't take these ideas to your boss or tuck them away for future use.

Who Are You?

Before starting any marketing or promotional program ask yourself some important questions. Take a close look at who you are and what you want to accomplish so you will know the best approach to market your individual, unique skills, discover your ultimate customers and how to get your message across to them. You are your business.

- What are your business and personal goals – for one year, three years, or five years?
- Who is your current customer base and are you satisfied with it?
- What is the name of your business? I highly recommend naming your business after yourself because it is "you" that you are promoting.
- Are your services/products going directly to the ultimate customer or do you handle job work for a variety of stores/clients?
- What special services, education and skills do you possess?
- What special equipment do you have, i.e., cad cam, laser welder, casting facilities?
- Why would someone use your company instead of the guy next door?
- How do you currently increase your customer base?
- Do you have custom design capabilities? Do you have a portfolio of past work?
- Why are you a bench jeweler? Is it the freedom to design your own lifestyle, live where you want, be with your kids, work with your hands, be a creative problem solver, be the boss, or because you are carrying on a thousand year old craft and tradition?

The Competition

Now ask yourself, who is your competition?

Not long ago, your competition was the person in the next town or down the street, but with the internet and one day mail service it makes someone two time zones away your direct competition. However, it goes without saying that being right on the spot where you can pick up and deliver or get instructions face-to-face is a bonus – that is a point to be emphasized when talking to current or potential customers. Your service is therefore more personalized, convenient, and doesn't cost to ship, saves trips to the post office and is more secure. Take a closer look at your competition:

- Who are they?
- Why do you consider them your competition?
- What services/products do they offer that you don't offer? What services to do you offer they don't?
- Why would someone use them and not you, and vice versa?
- Why should someone trust you to repair the family keepsake?
- How do they get their clients? Who are their clients? Do they advertise or promote themselves? How? Where?
- What do they charge?

It is always important to know your competition. You are in business and if you aren't knowledgeable about what they are doing and who they work with, I can assure you that they know this about you. I'm not talking industrial espionage, however being aware of what is happening in the world will give you a clearer vision of potential new clients or why there might be a possibility of losing someone to the competition. Where do you fit in?

Your Customer

Describe your customer.

- Is it a retail store or a neighborhood resident?
- Why are they your customer?
- Who feels confident enough with your skills and professionalism to trust their store's reputation on your work?
- Who trusts you with thousands of dollars of their jewelry?
- What do these customers have in common?

A Marketing Plan

All this information will help you design a marketing plan so you can reach a potential client base you haven't touched in the past. It is like traveling from Yakima, Washington to Camden, Maine without the use of a reliable map (or GPS). If you know where you are going you can get back on course if you make a little detour.

Write out your ideas and goals. Keep a file. Know where you want to go, how much it is going to cost and what you expect in return.

Research what other service-based businesses are doing to get their name in front of the public. Don't just confine your observations to the jewelry industry, there are lots of businesses which are promoting themselves (even something from the dry cleaning world might be an inspiration), what are they doing and how can you take a good idea and make it work for you?

With any type of marketing you want to spend as little money as possible and get the biggest bang for your buck. This is called ROI or Return on Investment. The less you spend and the more successful a strategy is, the higher the ROI.

Marketing

Below are some ideas you might try to creatively market and promote your business. You are only limited by your energy and time. Have fun with it.

1. Technology has changed everything. It is a current business maxim that if you don't have a website then you aren't in business. It makes you legitimate. Even if it is a short one page site, you must have a presence online.

2. Social networking is also new on the scene as far as marketing yourself. This means you can Twitter, Facebook, Link-In or Blog. It is a whole new world with a whole new vocabulary and it isn't going away. Social networking is not particularly about pushing your services but rather approaching current and potential clients from the point of view of educating and offering a service to the public. It keeps your name out there. This shift in networking or promoting yourself online is that traditionally a few passed down information to the many (such as in established large corporate TV, radio and print) now the many (you and me) share information with the many. It is an extraordinary transformation in thinking and approaching new markets and it should be the foundation of much of your "marketing." And the ROI makes it worth the effort. Learn as much as you can about this new medium as the dividends will be rewarding.

3. Teach a class. Write an article. Not just for the industry but for the public. Again, get your name out there. Tell the public how to take care of their jewelry so it doesn't end up on your bench for repair. Write about how to check the prongs on a diamond ring. Come up with helpful hints and tips. This will increase your presence and visibility in the industry as well as the public.

4. Provide a gift certificate the next time you are asked to donate something for a charity. This way the certificate recipient gets the privilege and opportunities to work directly with you to either repair or create a piece for them.

5. If you have a storefront consider having events that focus on repair, cleaning people's jewelry, teaching them how to care for their pieces, or finding out the materials used in a piece. Help them rediscover treasures already in their possession.

6. If you don't now, think about offering custom design services. You don't have to be a world-famous jewelry designer to create beautiful works a customer wants.

7. Offer a referral program. A current client refers someone to you for service, you give them a discount on their next repair or a gemstone or a pair of pearl earrings. It doesn't have to be much it just needs to say thank you and show that you appreciate their efforts and support.

8. Update your mailing list. As I tell people attending my classes, I want your mother's best friend and your best friend's mother on your list, especially if you have a storefront. I want your doctor, attorney, insurance agent on the list. They all sell you services and products, they know you and feel comfortable with you so let them know you are available to take care of their needs.

9. Have a brochure describing your services, skills and products. Once you decide to print something out, including your business card, make sure your materials have a consistent look, color, font, and message. Have an image that is reflective of you and your business.

I always recommend you design a logo, particularly if you are making jewelry to sell. You legally need to mark any piece with your logo, trademark or signature.

10. If you feel comfortable and secure, offer a studio tour to your best clients. People are always fascinated about how things are made and what goes into the process. Show them. One designer told me he came into the field by watching the local jeweler sit at his bench (behind glass) and perform miracles with his torch. Educate your public. Educate your stores. But always remember that security is paramount.

11. If you are thinking about spreading your name and services further than local clients, get in your car and take a sales trip. Like I mentioned earlier, with the aid of technology and one day services, you can have clients in other towns, states and time zones. Go out and look for your clients.

12. Don't hide the fact that you have a laser welder or can pave set diamonds like the best of them or that you have stone polishing skills. Let your customer know all the skills, education, and equipment you possess.

13. It sounds simple but be dependable and professional at all times. I have seen more careers ruined by unprofessional behavior. Take responsibility for your mistakes as well as your accomplishments. Make sure everything about your business is professional. If your darling daughter answers the phone and yells that it's for you, this isn't professional. Many bench jewelers work out of their homes, but that doesn't mean it still isn't a place of business and should be thought of as such at all times. Get a separate work number. This will also eliminate unwanted calls on Sunday afternoon.

14. Never, ever, ever walk out of your house without business cards on you. You are a walking, talking marketing tool. Take advantage of it. And make sure the cards you hand out are not dog-earred or dirty. Carry them in a zip lock bag if need be. Goodness knows all jewelers have plenty of these.

15. Join local business, civic and social organizations. You never know where your next client is going to come from. It is a well-known business concept that people do business with people they like. Make sure you are one of those.

16. Besides brochures and business cards, I would have some postcards printed so you can periodically mail them out to potential clients or current ones, reminding them you are in business and ready to offer your services.

17. Use the economy to your advantage. In difficult times, people would rather repair a piece of jewelry than buy a new one. Currently the trends in jewelry point to a slowdown in gold and platinum sales, so offer to repair a more precious piece instead of buying new. Make the most of the recession.

18. Educate your clients that repairing is more "green" than buying new or taking new raw materials out of the earth. In case you have been living in a cave, "green" is currently a powerful and useful buzz word.

19. One of my favorite things is "bartering." People who are really clever at it can get their hair cut for years, teeth worked on, and legal papers drawn up. It is a win-win situation for everyone involved and you can also develop new clients.

20. Handwrite a thank you note to your clients. Put yourself in their place, it is a

special thing to receive a "handwritten" note, it makes you feel appreciated.

21. Positive word of mouth and exceptional customer service are the strongest marketing tools you have in your arsenal. Your good reputation, dedication to extraordinary craftsmanship and professionalism are invaluable. Go out of your way to honor your clients. They make sure you stay in business. It is much easier to keep a current client than to go out and find new ones.

A few final words.

When you start marketing yourself and creatively going after new business you are selling your skills, educating your public and showing you are a professional in everything that you do, say and touch. Discover that marketing yourself can be a very creative part of your business. Take advantage of opportunities that come your way. Think outside that stupid box. Have a good time. Remember what you wrote down at the beginning of this article – why are you doing this.

If you don't love what you are doing, then what is the point?

Selling Custom Design Jewelry Online

Brad Simon

Selling your custom designed jewelry online can be a highly profitable venture or the biggest waste of time and money you have ever spent. The difference is generally in the approach you take in developing your online store. If you think that because sales are slow in your store you'll take a few days and put pictures of your jewelry on a website and the sales will start flowing in – forget about it. It just doesn't work like that.

We've all seen the Ads about internet millionaires who only work 2 hours a week and bring in millions of dollars a year while they cruise the world on their yacht. What those Ads don't tell you about is the hundreds of thousands of dollars they spend on salaries and independent contractors working on their website, so they don't have to.

Having an online store is like opening a second store across town or in a neighboring city. It's a lot of work, but if done right it can be profitable. Having an online store has its advantages over opening a second brick-n-mortar. The rent is extremely cheap, and there are virtually no security issues. An armed gunman is not going to break into your online store and clean out your safe! Its open 24 hours a day 7 days a week, 365 days a year. And although you still have to put in the work, you can do it when you're not busy at your store, late at night, on the weekends or on the balcony of some resort overlooking the ocean. Your work can be done anywhere you have high-speed Internet connection anytime of the day or night.

Shopping Cart

The heart of your online store is your shopping cart. How good your store will become, is in direct proportion to how good your shopping cart system is. A good shopping cart will provide you the secure server you need to protect your customer's information (something you do not want to do on your own unless you have an IT professional on your staff). It will track your sales telling you how the customers arrived at your online store so you can track the effectiveness of your marketing campaigns. It will allow you to featured products and suggested additional products available, send out auto responders, be fully customizable and much more. A good shopping cart will cost you $^{\$}50$ to $^{\$}150$ a month to use, but it is well worth the investment.

Marketing Your Online Store

Marketing your online store effectively is the key to online sales success. There are five basic methods to market your new online store.

1. Natural Search Marketing
2. Paid Website Ads
3. PPC (Pay Per Click)
4. Affiliate Sales
5. eMail Marketing

Natural Search Marketing

Natural Search Marketing, also known as Organic Search, is where someone types a word or phrase in Google or some other search engine and receives pages of website listings for that topic. You pay no commissions on sales, no fees to be listed, or for click-throughs. Getting a top listing on the search results pages is the most effective, low-cost marketing you can do on the internet. However, it does take work to get a top listing.

Two years ago, Local Search was started. This allowed geographical qualifiers to be included in search terms. This opened the door for retail jewelers to get top listings for jewelry related terms in their geographical area. This is what I mostly teach about and it is still fairly easy for a retail store to obtain these top listings for their city or area.

However, when you remove those geographical qualifiers it is a completely different story. To get a top listing for an online store you are competing with companies who have been working diligently for 10 to 15 years optimizing their websites and developing huge linking campaigns. In addition to keyword optimization and link development, Google and other search engines also look at the age of the website. Websites that are less than 2 years old will not get top search result listings on competitive keywords and phrases.

Because of this, a new online store cannot rely on Natural Search Marketing to bring them any new customers for the first couple of years. They do need to think in these terms and work diligently on keyword optimization and link development. After 2 to 3 years of consistently working at it when your website starts to mature, you will start to see results and you can very well replace some of the companies at the top. Especially if some of them become lax in their efforts or don't keep up with the ever-changing rules of Internet Marketing.

Paid Website Ads

There are a number of companies that you can purchase advertising space from and they will display your Ads on various related websites. Or you can contact website owners directly to purchase Ad space on their website. This type of Ad is generally a banner or video Ad.

These types of Ads are best for building brand awareness. For example, at Bench Media we sell advertising space on our websites for jewelry suppliers. This helps build brand awareness among bench jewelers for their products and services. However, this type of advertising does not generally produce high click-through rates.

Because of this, it is not the most productive advertising method for a new online store to generate customers. It is most effective for established companies to keep their name in front of their client base, and for new companies to start to develop their brand within their niche.

PPC (Pay Per Click)

Google's AdWords is the primary source for Pay Per Click advertising. With this program you set-up your Ads and Google places them on the side of the page in their search results and on other people's websites who's content is jewelry related. Whenever someone clicks on your Ad they're taken to your website and Google charges you a small fee. You don't pay anything for your Ad to be displayed, you only pay each time someone actually clicks on your Ad and visits your website.

This is the easiest and most effective method to get customers to a new online store. However, you need to monitor your Ad campaign closely, because you don't want to pay for traffic to your website that doesn't generate sales. You need to set-up several different AdWords campaigns and track each one on your website to see which Ad brings customers that are actually buying jewelry from your store and which are not. Then you can keep the best performing Ads. As well as eliminate the Ads that are just costing you money from people clicking on your Ad and then click the back button or clicking off to another website without purchasing.

Without diligent monitoring of your AdWords campaigns, you can waste a lot of money very fast and not generate any sales.

Affiliate Sales

Affiliate Sales is basic internet commission selling. You set-up an affiliate program and then people can join your program and place links to your store on their websites and email campaigns. When someone clicks on their link to your store and purchases a piece of jewelry for you, you pay them a commission on that sale. You do need to take time to develop your affiliate program, but you do not pay out any money unless a sale is made.

A good shopping cart has affiliate sales built in for you to create your own affiliate program. However, unless you have a large list of marketers eager to advertise your program, doing it yourself is generally not recommended.

There are many Affiliate program companies out there that will promote your affiliate program. Commission Junction www.cj.com and Link Share www.linkshare.com are two of the biggest. They have millions of online marketers looking for good affiliate programs to promote. If you are interested in this type of marketing, I would suggest visiting their websites and learn all you can about affiliate marketing. Look at and study their other jewelry companies they represent and see what type of commissions they pay and what promotions they offer. You have to give them a reason to promote your online store over some other store.

Affiliate programs are a great way to develop new customers for your online store, but it does take work. You need to create different banner Ads advertising your store and promotions. You need to develop sales copy and advertising materials for your affiliates to send out. You need to produce different promotions every quarter if not every month for your affiliates to promote you. You especially need new promotions for the top selling seasons such as Christmas, Mother's Day, and Valentine's Day.

eMail Marketing

eMail Marketing is by far the most effective and least costly method of advertising. Putting together a great email campaign takes a little bit of time, cost virtually nothing, and produces better open rates than direct mail and better click through rates than any other form on online marketing. Sending out an email about a special promotion to a well-developed list is like having your own printing press turning out dollar bills.

However, in order for you to do this effectively you must have a great email list! Obliviously you cannot do this when you are just starting out, but when you first set-up your online store you need to include a way to start receiving names and email addresses of potential clients and customers. Once you have a well-developed email list of prospects and clients you will find that this list is your most valuable asset, worth far more than anything else you own.

Conclusion

Once you have your online store in place and all the systems operational, running an online store is really just about marketing. You need to be continually developing new promotions to attract buyers. You need to up-date your website if not weekly at least monthly, to keep the search engines raising your ranking and your customers coming back. You need to continually write new advertising campaigns and test and monitor their effectiveness, refining and improving the best ones, then testing them again. You need to be constantly thinking about new ways to promote and market your online store. If this sounds like fun, then you will probably be successful if you are diligent in caring them out. However, if these types of activities don't excite you very much then it's doubtful your online store will produce anything but headaches for you.

The 3 Magical M's of Marketing

Brad Simon

In all forms of marketing there are Three Key Elements that you must carefully consider to be successful. And unfortunately, the old saying "two out of three aren't bad" does NOT hold true. Miss just one of these and your advertising will not only be less successful than it could have been but may actually lose you money costing you more than you receive in additional sales.

So, what are these Three Magical M's of Marketing? A long, long time ago a wise old master marketer told me that the key to all successful marketing is; "Finding where your customers are and stand in front of them with your message". Therein lies the three secrets of Marketing. They are:

1. **Use the Right Media**
2. **Create the Right Message**
3. **Target the Right Market**

Use the Right Media

As my wise marketing mentor told me, you must find where your customers are and stand in front of them. To be successful you need to know what media is most used by your ideal customer AND you must be able to use that media to get your message in front of them.

Centuries ago Town Criers would stand on the street corners yelling out messages to those passing by. Before the printing press was invented there was no other media choices. However, companies today have more choices of marketing media than ever before.

Do you realize that during the Great Depression, businesses produced more Millionaires than any other decade in history? Certainly, the past few decades has produced more through investments, but during the 1930's more business owners became millionaires than any other time in history.

How could this happen during such desperate times when so many were losing everything they owned? Well in great part, those companies that became outrageously successful did so by exploiting a new marketing media. During the 1920's radio became popular. In the 30's with little else to do, families would huddle around their radio to listen to stories that were broadcast, and to President Roosevelt deliver his Fireside Chats.

During the 1960's a similar experience occurred with television, and today there is an even greater phenomena happening in media. **We Are Now Living in the Single Biggest Culture Shift in History!**

And no, I'm not talking about the Internet! (Although the internet did make this shift possible)

How to Effectively Reach Today's Consumer

During the past decade, two different media have seen an explosion in growth, going from birth to consumer dominance in an unheard-of short time frame. As these two media merged over the past couple of years a Perfect Storm has formed for marketers to reach consumers like never seen before.

In 2007 Apple released the first iPhone and Google and Microsoft released their platforms soon after. Cellphone carriers pushed the new smartphone onto consumers as their old contract expired and a new phone was needed. As a result, Smartphones saturated the market faster than any electronic devise in history.

Today you cannot go anywhere without seeing numerous people on their phones. At the simplest sound of a beep or a few musical notes, people will interrupt what they are doing to see what their phones want. It doesn't matter if they are in the middle of a conversation, eating a meal, or driving down the street, out comes their phone. After all it is "Smart", so it knows better than we do, Right?

The second media, Social, started earlier than smartphones with websites like LinkedIn, Myspace, Friendster, and Twitter in the late 1990's and early 2000's. However, it did not gain real traction until Facebook finally switched to open registration in September 2006 from being strictly students of select universities.

During the same time frame that smartphones took over our lives, Social Media went from 'Geeks Only' to dominating our culture. Today more time is spent on Social Media Platforms than any other single activity including playing video games. In 2014 Social Media referred more traffic to websites than Search Engines, the only purpose the later serves. Facebook alone now outperforms Google in this task. 2015 has seen a continual decrease in search activity and an increase in social.

The Mobile-Social Revolution

While integration of Social Platforms on Mobile was slow at first, the past two years has seen total incorporation. Mobile Smartphones power our lives and Social is the [#]1 activity while on them. Facebook is not only the most downloaded app on mobile, it is the most frequently used app as well consuming 1 of every 5 minutes spent on mobile devises. Mobile Facebook users check their Newsfeed on average 14 times a day!

This merging of Social and Mobile has created what is now called the Mobile-Social Revolution. These two forces have created the Perfect Storm for marketers! Never before can you reach more consumers with your marketing message so easily, so cheaply, and so frequently.

Facebook Ad Platform

While you must have a Facebook Business Page to access their Ad Platform, Facebook's Ad Manager is a separate entity. Over the past two years Facebook has completely redesigned their ad platform which is administered from their Texas office. No other Facebook employees works on ads except those in this office and this office only works on the ad platform. Facebook has kept it completely separate from other operations.

Early this year Facebook rolled out their Ad Network to all advertisers. App developers can choose to place Facebook ads in their mobile app. Any business can now have certain types of their ads seen in any mobile app including video games, business tools, reference or any other type of mobile app.

In addition, Facebook recently announced they will be adding paid advertising this Fall to their mobile app Instagram. Rather than creating a separate ad platform, Instagram Ads will only be available through the Facebook Ad Manager.

This Christmas season, stores will be able to have their ads displayed in Facebook's Newsfeed, on Instagram, and a variety of other mobile apps, simply by creating one Ad in Facebook Ad Manager.

Today retailers can find more customers and present their message to them with Mobile-Social easier and more effectively than any other media available today. Currently Facebook's Ad Manager is the leader in providing low cost advertising across this platform.

Creating the Right Message

Of the 3 this is the most difficult to accomplish well and needs for us to spend the most time on. However, for too many jewelers, this aspect is almost an afterthought. More time is spent on the product or service offered, the sale or event, the media selection, the advertising budget, or other concerns. The actual content of the advertisement is often thrown together with little thought. Material is used from previous ads or content copied from someone else. As a result, our marketing is far less successful than it could be.

Why Your Message Matters

From the beginning of time until the year 2003, five billion gigabytes of information was published. Today five billion gigabytes of information is published every 10 minutes! The amount of information that took all of history up until 2003 to be published, is being created and published in less time than it will take you to read this article. The Information Superhighway has created Information Overload.

In 1960, every US citizen was exposed to around 1,500 advertising messages per day, by 1990 this number had doubled to 3,000 messages per day and to 5,000 messages per day in the year 2000. Today consumers are bombarded with over 15,000 advertising messages every day.

Your message must cut through the marketing clutter. Our brains cannot truly process that much information. The vast majority of marketing messages we are exposed to every day goes by without notice. We have become immune to information and especially marketing. We tune it out. Only a very small percentage of the information we are subjected to is noticed, much less absorbed and given meaningful thought to.

Stop the Scroll

There is so much information thrown at us today that consumers could not read it all even if they spend all day reading. As a result, they quickly scroll through their Newsfeed stopping to read only what seems interesting to them.

The content of your marketing message, the images and text, must Grab Their Attention and Stop the Scroll. If not, they will zoom past and never know they had been exposed to it.

Create the Desire

Here is where most Social Media advertising fails!

A cute baby picture or funny pet picture can grab consumer's attention. But if the image is not related to your product or service it will not create a desire to own the product or use the service.

The right message should link the use of your products and services with their innermost wants and cravings. It should trigger an emotion within them and cause them to believe that their life will be better if only they had what you offer.

As mentioned earlier, there is stiff competition for consumer's time and attention. It is hard enough to grab their attention, but once you do if you do not connect with them and create this desire they will quickly move on to the next item.

Compel Them to Action

Once the desire to own your product or use your service is created, you must motivate them to take action. There are a lot of women who desire to own and wear a nice piece of jewelry. But if they are never compelled to come into a jewelry store and take out their credit card and purchase it, the desire does not benefit the jeweler.

You need a strong CTA (Call To Action) that tells them specifically what to do. 'Come in Today' and 'Call Us Now' are both examples of a strong CTA. They are short, direct, and there is no question as to what you want consumers to do. In addition, they both add a sense of urgency.

'Go Ahead – Indulge Yourself' is another effective form of CTA. While not directly telling them to contact your business as in the above examples, it gives the consumer permission to make the purchase. People in general are apprehensive of being seen as self-indulgent, uneasy to make a self-purchase. Receiving reassurance that it is OK, even from a complete stranger, is often all that is needed to bring them into your store.

Forget About the Click

Ever since the first internet link ad was created, Marketers have obsessed over Clicks, Click Thru Rates, and website traffic. And, for an online store, these measurements are all important. However, for brick-n-mortar stores it is not website traffic that matters. In-store traffic is the only measure local retailers should concern themselves about.

A recent study by Data Logix revealed that over 99% of people who purchased products in a brick-n-mortar store never clicked on an online ad.

Unless the goal of your ad is solely for prospecting and you have a strong capture mechanism to gather email addresses on your website for future email marketing, don't waste your time and marketing dollars creating ads to send people there. Consumer's attention span is short and the space in your ad is limited. You will be far better served if you wisely spend that space on driving customers to your store and forget about getting clicks on your ad. Get Their Feet Thru The Door, not their eyeballs on your website!

To create a compelling message that grabs consumer's attention, creates a desire for your products and services, and motivates them to shop with you is a daunting task. Especially considering the limited space most advertising provides for you. In spite of this, taking the time to improve the content in your messages often makes the difference between an average marketing message that produces mediocre results and one that is outrageously successful.

Target the Right Market

In today's Information Age targeting your marketing has become imperative. Yet most small business owners don't understand the importance of it nor know how to properly implement it.

Why Targeting Matters

As mentioned earlier, today's consumers are bombarded with over 15,000 advertising messages every day. Consumers quickly filter out what they are interested in from the irrelevant. If a marketing message does not apply to them at that very moment, they pass over it without giving it second thought.

A shotgun approach to marketing still used by some companies hasn't worked effectively for years. There was a time when you could broadcast your message successfully to everyone. Those that were in need of your product or service took action. Knowing they may have a future need for it, the rest would store the information away for future use.

That approach simple doesn't work anymore. So much information is thrown at us daily that we can barely keep up with what is relevant, much less remember something that we might need in an uncertain future.

In today's culture even a rifle approach is too broad and little better than shotgun marketing. You need a laser scope to zero in on a precise target. For example:

Engagement Ring advertisements targeting all men would be a shotgun approach. But an ad with a man proposing on bended knee would have no interest to a married man. Nor would it appeal to a single man who is not dating. In fact, reminding him he cannot get a steady girlfriend may cause a negative impression of your store.

A rifle approach would be to target the ad with the man proposing only to single men in a serious relationship. Then create a different ad with a romantic couple appealing to married men with the message to upgrade her diamond for an anniversary. And don't show any Engagement Ring Ads to single men not in a relationship.

While more successful than the shotgun approach to marketing, this rifle targeting is still too broad for today's sophisticated consumer. A small inexpensive diamond engagement ring may be an insult to a successful businessman. You certainly don't want to try to encourage him to upgrade his wife's diamond with a picture of a ring smaller than hers. On the other hand, while you want to stretch their budget, showing rings far above what someone can afford could turn them off. Rather than creating a desire to do business with you, they see you as condescending and pretentious.

A laser approach to targeting begins with the basic demographics of rifle marketing but adds advanced demographics as well. Financial data such as annual household income and net worth, as well as the age of the consumer should all be considered. But don't stop there. Today's marketer has advanced Psychographics at their disposal as well. You can precisely target a person's likes, interest, beliefs, and values.

Does the consumer prefer a more traditional appearance, or would a modern design fit their style? Do they want a subdued sophisticated look or are they bold and flashy? Do they prefer white or yellow gold, or is platinum the only thing that will do? Do they want a traditional diamond for their engagement ring or a classic of sapphire or ruby? Round, Emerald, Heart Shaped, or is a Princess Cut her fancy?

Knowing what the customer wants and desires, allows you to precisely match your marketing to them. When they see that picture of the perfect ring along with your message crafted just for them you will create that burning desire that can only be quenched by a visit to your store for the ultimate purchase.

A Targeting Platform for Small Businesses

By now many of you may be thinking that this all sounds great, but where can you find such detailed information on consumers? And if you can find it, how is a small business able to afford such advanced targeting?

Well I have Great News for you! There is an advertising platform that is working hard for SMBs (Small and Medium Businesses). This platform has developed the most comprehensive database of Demographic and Psychographic information ever compiled on consumers.

What is this Miracle Advertising Platform?

It may surprise you, but it is the Ad Manager inside of Facebook. With Facebook's Ad Manager you can display paid advertising on the two largest Social Media networks, Facebook and Instagram. In addition, through their Ad Network you can place native ads within third-party Mobile Apps. With over 1.5 million businesses advertising on Facebook it is now the largest mobile advertising platform edging out Google's AdMob.

However, what sets Facebook Ad Manager apart from all the rest is not the enormous number of consumers you can reach with Facebook advertising, nor the vast array of different Ad Objectives or types of ads that you can create. The most impressive aspect of Ad Manager is the mammoth database of consumer information available to advertisers to laser focus your marketing to a hyper-targeted group of consumers. Never before has such Demographic and Psychographic information ever been assembled for small and medium businesses to use.

To begin with, Facebook has all the basic demographic information their 1.4 billion users entered in their Personal Profiles. Then Facebook monitors all your activities on their social network. Every time you post something to your timeline Facebook records what you posted. When you 'Like' a post or click on a picture, video, or article; Facebook records your interest. For the past 10 years this information has been carefully compiled and cataloged in Facebook's database. This alone provides more information on consumers Likes, Interest, and Behaviors than any competing marketing platform.

As if that wasn't enough information, Facebook went out and partner with the 3 Largest Data Services; Epson, Acxion, and Datalogix. If you wanted to send a mailing to people in your target zip codes with a certain household income, this is the type of company your mail service would buy the list from. Facebook compiles the complete database of these three services. Just this composite list would make Facebook the largest data service. But they then combine that data with their own list creating an unprecedented source of consumer information for marketers to use. It provides even the smallest of businesses unbelievable resources to target their advertising. For as little as one dollar a day you can advertise through Facebook Ad Manager with access to all these advanced hyper-targeting metrics.

When Your Marketing contains the Perfect Message, presented on the Proper Media, targeting the Ideal Market how can you fail? You can transform your ordinary ads into Outrageously Successful ones and see a greater ROI on your advertising.

Follow Your Customer's Lead - Text Them!

Brad Simon

Mobile phones are used by your customers for text messaging more than voice phone calls and Internet access combined. There are now over 276 million mobile wireless subscribers in the U.S., which is more than 89% of the population. The latest Forrester Research statistics show that more than 2.2 trillion text messages are sent in the U.S. every year. That equates to over six billion text messages sent every day, in the United States alone.

Texting Is Cross-Generational

Texting is a teenager's most common form of communication. Pew Internet Research reports that 75% of teenagers in the U. S. text, and on average they each text 60 messages a day. That is more than social networks, phone calls, and face-to-face communication combined.

Americans ages 20-29 are the most frequent text messagers. They send and receive an average of nearly 88 text messages per day, compared to only 17 daily phone calls. The 45 to 64 age demographic is the fastest growing text messagers with the largest increase in text messages sent over last year.

While it's true that the number of text messages decline with older demographics (as well as overall frequency of all communication), texting is still the most frequently used communication avenue. Those over 65 text 4.7 times more frequently than calling. A recent TIME Mobility Poll revealed that 32% of all respondents over 65 even prefer to communicate by text rather than phone with people they know very well.

How Does this Affect Small Business Owners?

Mobile Text Message Marketing for small business owners is the fastest growing advertising medium today. Newspapers are in decline, radio stations are hurting, direct mail does not produce returns as in the past, and Yellow Pages are almost extinct. They are not producing advertising results like they used to because consumers today are using their smart phones and other mobile devices all day long, every day. You know that to reach your customers you must advertise to them where they are, at that moment. Text messaging allows direct and instant contact with your customers and potential customers and, more importantly, will produce increased sales.

The Mobile Marketing Association states that more than half of all national brands had shifted their focus from advertising with traditional media to mobile marketing in 2012 and many more plan to do so this year. Over 40% have already started text messaging, and 2013 marketing budgets include up to 25% for mobile with many of these national brands.

Now you can do more than just endure the national chains in your market area who work hard to take away your customers. You can take them on head to head, leveling the playing field. You now have the ability to get your customers on a list and entice them to remain your loyal customer with rewards and great offers.

The cost of text marketing has dropped significantly over the last few years, so you will not have to invest 25% of your marketing budget on mobile to compete. You can start a mobile marketing campaign for less than $40 per month with many text message marketing companies.

Welcome to Text Message Marketing: The New ROI Generation Machine

All jewelers want the same thing from their marketing. They want to establish a great brand in their company name, entice more consumers to visit their jewelry store and develop a loyal customer base for repeat business. While websites, social media and traditional marketing are helpful, consumer behaviors have evolved to the point that these tactics simply do not generate the ROI they once did.

Text Message Marketing is successful for numerous reasons. Consider that Text Messages are:

- **Permission Based** – Customers want to receive text messages and show that by opting in. They prove they are interested in you and are waiting to receive value-based messages from you, whether it's an announcement of new jewelry, a discount coupon or other informative message.

- **Prompt** – 98% of people will open their text messages within 3 minutes of receiving it, which helps to increase your engagement. This is the only marketing tool that encourages immediate action.

- **Proficient** – The redemption rate for Mobile Coupons is 10 times higher than traditional coupons. 50% of consumers receiving text messages from retailers have made a purchase based on messages received. There is not a more effective marketing media today.

- **Proven** – An American Express study found 84% of small businesses that implemented text marketing have seen a resulting increase in new business activity.

- **Personal** – When customers agree to receive your company's texts, they are welcoming you into their personal circle normally reserved for friends and family. This creates a sense that your company is friendly and trustworthy rather than a cold corporation. Use this to your advantage when writing your messages so that they come across in a pleasant personal manner.

- **Preferred** – Consumers now use their mobile phone for text messages more than voice and Internet access combined. 66% of U.S. mobile customers say they prefer offers from stores they do business with by text message rather than any other media.

- **Profitable** – At 3 to 5 cents per contact, Text Messaging services offer one of the least expensive forms of advertising. And when the high response rate is factored in, Text Messages produce the lowest cost per sale that no other form of advertising can even come close to.

Text messages are commonly forgotten about when marketing options are considered, but it remains the quickest and best way to communication. Your customers love to text so use that to your advantage. **Jewelers who don't look for ways to integrate text message into their marketing to communicate with customers and grow their business will soon find that they are left behind.**

Customer Texting Etiquette

Text messaging has grown from a niche form of communication to a powerful tool to connect with customers regardless of their age group. You now have the ability to reach hundreds or even thousands of customers quickly and easily through mass messages called Text Blast. However, the ease of text programs to send mass communications should be tempered with good etiquette and respect for your customers.

Clear Opting-In

You know that first impressions are very important, and it is especially important when texting your customers. Texting from businesses still evokes apprehension in some people and you don't want to catch them off guard. Be certain your customers have specifically opted-in to your texting program.

If your customer has given you their cell phone number for other reasons, such as to notify them their jewelry repair is finished, do not assume you can start texting them regularly with your offers. Doing so may irritate them and damage their trust in you. Additionally, they could report you causing your account to be closed and possibly incur hefty fines.

Set Your Boundaries

You should advise your customers of what they can expect when they opt-in to your list. You can do this at the time of sign up or with your first text. You will alleviate any worries of being flooded with messages they don't want by telling them your plans. Being up front may even make them excited for your next message. Don't be too specific; give yourself a margin for error.

Be Respectful

Text messages are opened when they are received. One of the fastest ways to upset customers and have them unsubscribe is to send them messages at the wrong time. Wake them up at 2 am to share a coupon and not only will they unsubscribe, but you may lose them as a customer! The most appropriate time to send texts are between 10am and 8pm. However, avoid rush-hour. You don't want your customers trying to read your message while driving.

Think Beyond Advertising

You want your text messaging to have an incentive for your customer to read them. If all you do is advertise, you are not rewarding your customer for signing up. Proper etiquette rewards your customer for trusting you with their information and allowing you to send messages to them. Sending a coupon or exclusive offer unavailable by other means on a regular basis is one example. When people know they will get special incentives it encourages sign-ups and improves retention. Plus, they will actually be drawn to your jewelry store to make a purchase.

Provide Exit Strategies

You must make opting out simple. Anti-spam regulations require clear opt out information in every bulk text message you send. More importantly, people become aggravated when they cannot figure out how to unsubscribe. When you offer clear instructions to unsubscribe it shows your customer that they are your first priority. It sends a message about your integrity. Easy unsubscribe is more than good etiquette, it's good business.

For all those jewelry store owners and marketers who use text messaging as part of their marketing campaign, great for you! You already know how your customers prefer to receive valuable offers and information regarding their favorite jeweler. You know that you are more likely to see success and more sales. If you don't already use Text Messaging, I encourage you to explore ways to add it into your marketing campaign today.

Pricing

Quote Worth Re-Quoting

"Pricing is the exchange rate you put on all the tangible and intangible aspects of your business. Value for cash."

— *Patrick Campbell*

Value Based Pricing part 1

Brad Simon

Do you remember the song How Much Is that Doggie in the Window that we sang way back in our childhood?

How much is that doggie in the window?
The one with the 74aggle tail.
How much is that doggie in the window?
Oh I do hope that doggie for sale.

Ever since retail began people have wondered how to price their products and services. Pricing decisions are perhaps the single largest determining factor as to whether a company makes a profit or not and how much of a profit it will make. If you set your prices too low, you will end up with a loss. If you set your prices too high, customers will go elsewhere to purchase the product.

Services, such as jewelry repair, can be even more difficult to price than products. Services are non-tangible; you cannot touch or hold them. You can see, hold, and feel a ring but you cannot see, hold, or feel a ring sizing. This creates pricing difficulties, as you do not have tangible things like stones or metal to base a price on. Rather than being able to see advantages such as the number or size of stones customers have to depend on such ambiguous characteristics as reputation or image of the person providing the service.

Services are also non-transferable. A ring sizing cannot be returned. You cannot transfer a ring sizing to another ring, nor give it away or hand it down to another person. Services are also non-storable. You cannot stock up on ring sizings during the slower summer months and have them available for the rush during the Christmas season.

In addition, with the services you perform you do not have a manufacturer's cost or suggested retail price to work with, as you do with the jewelry and watch products in our stores. This all leads to problems when we try to set prices for our jewelry repair services.

Pricing Myths

In the jewelry industry, there are two myths that flourish among retailers as to setting prices for jewelry repairs. This further complicates the already difficult process of setting repair prices. The first myth is that you should set your prices based on what others charge.

There is a story of a man who worked in a factory. He lived on the opposite side of town from the factory, and every day he would walk through town on his way to work. Each morning as he past though the downtown shopping area he would stop in front of the finest jewelry store and stare in the front window. He would gaze through the window for a moment, look at his watch, and then continue to work.

The storeowner grew so perplexed by this man's behavior that one day he went outside to meet him. He said that every day he saw him staring though his window and he was curious as to what he was looking at. The man told the storeowner that it was his job to blow the noon whistle every day at the factory, and he took his job very seriously. So, every day he would stop in front of the store because it was the finest jewelry store in town. He would look through the window at the stores clock and check his watch to make certain his watch was correct. This way he was assured that he would blow the noon whistle precisely at 12 o clock.

The storeowner told the man he admired his dedication to his job. In fact, the storeowner said, you are so accurate in performing your job, that for years we have set the clock in our store by his noon whistle.

After years of carrying out this ritual, is there any way that either of them had a clue as to what the correct time really was?

For years, jewelry store owners have set their prices for jewelry repairs by calling other stores in town and then set their prices, based on what the other stores charge. If you use this method to set prices, you are setting your prices based on stores who have most likely called you sometime in the past to see what you charge and then set their prices based on what you charge. After years of carrying out this ritual, is there any way that any jeweler has a clue as to what the correct price should be for jewelry repairs?

You cannot set your prices correctly in your store just by calling the other stores in town and setting your prices accordingly.

The second myth to setting jewelry repair prices is to set your prices based solely on your cost.

A real problem develops when we set our prices based solely on our cost. At the end of the year we evaluate our jeweler's performance and based on the shops income we determine if we can afford to give our jewelers a raise. Now, if we set our prices based on what we pay our jewelers, and pay our jewelers based on what we collect from the prices we set, is there any way either can be correct?

In addition, isn't it obvious that if our income (the prices we charge) is based on what we pay our jeweler there will never be extra money to give our jewelers a raise? Commissions do not solve this problem either. If you set your price, and the commission the jeweler receives, based on how long it should take the jeweler to perform the work then the only way for them to make more money is to do the work faster than they should be doing it.

Unless we set our prices based on the value of the services, we provide we will never have the money to pay the kind of wages that reflect the value of our jeweler's labor. When we as an industry start charging prices based on the value of the service we provide, not only will the store profits increase, but we will finally be able to provide the wages to our jewelers comparable with the wages paid in other skilled professions.

When you determine the value of your services you will then know how much to price that doggie in the window.

In the next article, we will look at methods to help you determine what your customers believe the value of your repair services to be.

Value Based Pricing part 2

Brad Simon

In the last article we looked at two myths to setting prices on your jewelry repairs. This month we will look at a preferable method to determining what to charge.

Imagine for a moment, that there is no money. You cannot buy anything; you must barter. For example, if you need the oil changed in your car and your mechanic needs a ring sized, you could size his ring in exchange for the oil change in your car. Everybody would be happy – until you drove 3,000 miles and needed another oil change. You return to your mechanic only to find he does not have another ring that needs to be sized. So, you find a window washer who needs a ring sized, and you size his ring. In exchange, he washes your mechanic windows, who in exchange, changes the oil in your car. Once again, everybody is happy, until…

As an alternative to this trading system, man devised money to simplify his life. (I bet you never thought of money as simplifying your life, did you?) You size your window washer ring and in exchange, he pays you an amount of money equivalent to the value of the service you provide. You then go to your mechanic for your oil change and pay him an amount of money equivalent to the value of the service he provides. Your mechanic then goes to your window washer and he has his windows washed and pays him an amount of money equivalent to the value of the service he provides. Once again, everybody is happy. That is of course, as long as everybody has set their prices correctly.

You see the ONLY reason to set a price is to establish the value for the product or service being rendered. Then a fair exchange of your service for their money can be made. And there is only one person who decides what the value of your services are – and it is not you – it is your customer. Your customer decides the value of your services and whether or not it is worth parting with their hard-earned cash in exchange for it.

Pubilius Syrus, a first century Roman writer stated: A thing is worth whatever the buyer will pay for it. Old Pubilius was my kind of guy. He was able to boil down the essence of pricing to 11 words. The Internal Revenue Service and Treasury Regulations is a little wordier. Here is an excerpt from Revenue Procedures 66-49. Fair market value is the price at which the property or service would change hands between a willing buyer and a willing seller, if neither one is under any compulsion to buy or sell… Sadly, over the years we have forgotten Pubilius Syrus advice when we set our prices. All we think about is the second part of the Treasury Regulations – the willing seller. How much am I willing to sell my services for? How much does it cost me? How little can I sell it for? Instead we should be asking: How much is MY customer willing to pay for my services?

You see, the ONLY reason a doctor or lawyer can receive more money for their services than most other people, is because their clientele believes their time is more valuable. In order to set your prices correctly you need to find out how much your clientele perceives your time is worth. When you find this out, then you will be able to price your shop services properly. There are a number of methods you can use to find this information including:

Ask

We all have a group of people we feel comfortable discussing business with. Ask them to review your prices. See what they feel is the maximum they would be willing to pay for your services.

Surveys

Compile a short survey asking various questions concerning marketing and advertising. Then include questions about prices. For example, What is the maximum you would pay for ___? Add in various repair services such as: sizing a ring, repairing a chain, retipping a prong, and replacing a post on an earring.

Labor Rate Comparison

Many times a customer will come into your store paying you what you charge for a repair. Then, they leave and spend two to three times that per hour to have their electronic equipment, or cars repaired. An excellent method to determine what your customers will spend for your services is to consider what they are spending for labor on similar work to be performed. What is the going labor rate in your area? This is not what the laborers are being paid but what the stores are charging for labor. Some industries to consider include, Accounting, Appliance Repair, Auto Mechanic, Carpentry, Cleaning Services, Commercial Artists, Computer Repair, Electricians, Electronic Repair, Graphic Artists, Plumbing, Lawn Services, and Shoe Repairing.

Service Comparison

Another excellent method to use is to compare what your customers willingly pay for other similar services and then price your services correspondingly. Consider such items as: a doctor office visit, an oil change in a car, painting a room in a house, having a book re-bound, filing tax returns, tune-up of a lawnmower, and repairing a toaster. For example, an oil change for your car takes about the same time as sizing a ring. The cost of the oil and filter is about the same as the gold needed for sizing. However, the skill level of the high school kid changing your oil is lower than your goldsmith. Therefore, the oil change has a slightly lower value than the ring sizing, and you can reasonably price your sizing slightly higher than what your customers pay to have their oil changed.

Test Pricing

To do this, raise the prices on all repairs for a period of time. At the end of the period, raise them again. Gradually raise the price on each item until you receive significant price resistance. When you receive price resistance on an item do not raise that price anymore but continue to raise prices on the other items. When significant price resistance is received on each item, you have reached the peak market price for your store.

What method you use is not nearly as important as that you find out the information from your customers. The clientele in each store perceives the value of those services differently. Therefore, management in each store must make their own pricing decisions based on their clienteles perceived value of the services they provide from their shop.

When you know what value YOUR clientele places on the services you provided, and therefore what prices they would be willing to pay for them, then you will know how much to price that doggie in the window.

3 C's of Effective Pricing

Brad Simon

In 1996, with the World Olympics only three hours away my wife and I took our two boys to experience the excitement and the multitude of world cultures. As you know, when you travel with children, there is something you must do. You must eat at McDonalds at least once. I think it is a law somewhere. It does not matter that here at the Olympics there is a vast array of food vendors with varieties of food from all over the world, we ate hamburgers with exactly the same ingredients and prepared using exactly the same process that McDonald hamburgers are made in Spartanburg. But do you know what? McDonalds charges more for that same hamburger in Atlanta, than they do in Spartanburg.

My wife is from Chicago, and we frequently travel there to visit my in-laws. If you are ever in Chicago, check out the Rock & Roll McDonalds. You don't even need to have children. It is right across the street form the Hard Rock Café just north of downtown. They have life size statues of all four of the Beatles along with other rock and roll memorabilia. But take along your wallet! Chicago has Atlanta beat. The price they charge for that very same hamburger is out of sight.

A few years ago, we traveled to New York City. With Broadway, Time Square, the Empire State Building, the Statue of Liberty, and FINE DINING, I thought I was finally free from the McDonalds law. Do you know what the very first thing my boys saw? Right there in the middle of Time Square is a child's dream come true; a two story tall McDonalds. Now, I know that you can't believe this, but they charge even more than Chicago for the very same hamburger.

Now, there is a very good reason McDonalds charges more in these places for the same hamburger. It is because they CAN charge more. They are in a different market area, and they can charge higher prices because that market allows them to.

The jewelry business is no different. When setting prices for your jewelry repairs, it does not matter what some guy in Atlanta, Chicago, or New York charges. Their market area is different and your prices need to be different from theirs.

However, just because you may not be in a large market does not necessarily mean that you have to charge rock bottom prices.

My sister lives in a small community of just a couple thousand people. The one grocery store in town has some of the highest prices I have ever seen. My sister pays more for groceries there, than my in-laws do in Chicago. This storeowner knows that my sister and the other residents will pay his higher prices rather than traveling 40 miles to a larger town.

Sometimes if you are in a smaller town, you can charge higher prices. However, other times the smaller towns need to charge the lower prices and the higher prices are found in the bigger cities.

In order for you to know what you can charge, you must consider three essential ingredients to establishing proper prices on your services. I call them **the 3 C's of Effective Pricing.**

They are:
- **Cost**
- **Competition**
- **Customers**

Cost

When setting prices on your services you must first and foremost consider your cost to provide that service. You cannot stay in business long, if you charge less than what it cost you to perform that service.

It is important that you figure all your cost involved at your store. It cost McDonalds more money to operate on Time Square than it does in Spartanburg SC. Now I know minimum wage is the same, but it cost more to build and maintain a building. Advertising and other expenses are all greater.

The jewelry industry is no different. Your costs are different from jewelers in other cities as well as different from the jeweler down the street. You cannot set proper prices in your store simply by charging what they charge.

You must exactly and completely calculate all cost involve. This includes the Cost of Labor (including taxes and benefits in addition to salaries), Cost of Materials, and Shop Overhead (tools, shop supplies, etc.). Then, add to this cost your normal store mark-up to cover the salespersons time, advertising, rent, insurance, and all other normal retail expenses.

When establishing your prices DO NOT be ashamed of making a profit on your labor. There is nothing immoral or unethical in making a fair profit when performing a legal service and helping a customer overcome a problem they have. If a customer comes to you with a broken chain, and you help them with their problem by fixing their chain, there is nothing wrong with charging an amount that will not only cover your cost but provide you with a fair profit.

Each of us has a different idea of what FAIR amounts to. By working through the next two steps will help you establish not only what you think is fair, but more importantly what your customers believe is fair.

Reason for Cost Based Pricing

It is important that you figure all your cost involved at your store. Many stores have their price lists from years or decades ago and have only changed prices with an across the board price increase every few years or when the price of metal goes up.

One store that I worked at did an intensive price study. This store loved the Easy-Lock clasp for neck chains. We would order these two or three dozen at a time and put them on most all chains that we sold and recommended them to almost every customer that brought a chain in for repair. As a result of the price study we found that our cost to buy the clasp was higher than the retail price we were charging. We were losing money just on the purchase of the clasp not even figuring anything for my labor to solder the clasp onto the chain. No one at the store had ever taken the time to look at the invoice to see what we were paying for the clasp. We charged what we had always charged and had added a little every other year for a "Cost of Living Increase".

Very few jewelry stores have taken the time to sit down and figure out what their cost involved are in performing the repairs. As a result, many store prices are well below their cost. Unless you sit down and take the time to figure all your cost on each repair you will never know what the minimum you can charge and still make a profit.

Competition

I take no issue with any man that charges less for his labor than me. For who would be more expert than he in what his work is really worth?

As important as analyzing your cost is, it is only the first step in setting prices. You must next examine your competition and determine your position in the industry. You need to look at items such as quality, turn-around-time, types of repairs you perform, and how they compare to others within the industry.

For example: A poor ring sizing may cost just as much as an exceptional one, but that does not mean that it should be priced the same. An exceptional job should cost more than a marginal one.

Now you may say that the jeweler who does the better work has a higher skill level and is paid more. Therefore, the cost is higher for him to do the sizing than the lower skilled worker doing the poorer job. However, that is not always true.

The more skilled worker may not only do better work, he may do it faster. He may be paid more per hour but by finishing the job in less time, the cost to do the job may be the same as the other jeweler doing mediocre work.

Because of this, in addition to determining your cost, you must analyze your position in the industry. Are you the Rolex of the repair industry for your community or the Timex? Or are you somewhere in between, a good middle of the road guy? Knowing your place in the hierarchy of the industry will help you set your prices.

There are hamburger stands that sell hamburgers at a lower price than McDonalds. There are also many restaurants charging more for a hamburger than they do. McDonalds is neither the cheapest hamburger in town, nor the most expensive. They understand their position in the hierarchy of the restaurant industry, and they set their prices accordingly.

To set your prices properly, you need to do the same. To do this, it is important to study and analyze our competition. Not to copy their prices, but to gain insights and information that is vital in establishing correct prices in our stores. Often our customers know more about what our competition offers than we do. They know; how well they do their work; how long it takes; and how much they charge. This puts us at a disadvantage when we try to sell them on why we should do their repairs and attempt to justify why we charge what we charge.

You need to know where your prices fit in the overall pricing structure of your area. If you have an image as a quality store but charge the lowest prices in town, you are sending mixed messages to your customers as well as losing potential revenues.

Methods to Determine Position in the Industry

Call the Competition

The more stores you contact the better your results will be. When comparing all the stores in your area over a broad range of jobs a truer picture of the market is established. You will find some stores are higher on some repairs and lower on others. You will find some stores charging extremely low prices and others charging two or three times as much. These are not always the stores you would expect to be charging those prices.

A Word of Caution, Do Not use this as your ONLY means used to setting your price, as is often the practice. You should use this only as a guideline. This is one tool of many to help you set your prices.

Shop the Competition

Have someone take jewelry to stores in your area for repair. The amount of money you pay them for these repairs is minimal to the amount of information you can gain. Such as prices, turn-around-time, quality of work, etc.

Industry Standards

In developing the Bench Jewelers Certification Program, Jewelers of America established certain standards for what different repairs should look like. Compare your work with those standards. Do you perform your work at a level above those standards? If so you can price your work higher.

Networking

Attend conferences, shows, and other trade events and talk with other jewelers. This is an excellent way to see how others in the industry perform their work and how yours stacks up.

Items to Consider

Quality

Because of their intangible nature, services can be even more difficult to price than products. The tendency for customers to use price as an indicator of quality, is more pronounced. Consumers equate high price with high quality and that a low price means low quality. People believe you get what you pay for.

When pricing repairs and custom work from your shop you can use quality to your advantage. This is true if you provide superior craftsmanship or higher quality materials than your competition.

You can also charge a higher price if you use higher quality materials. Some examples are: using plumb solder instead of repair solder, retipping with metal instead of building up solder on the prong, using white gold alloyed with palladium instead of nickel, and using heads with heavier prongs.

Point out these differences to the customer. They need to know the quality advantages in labor and materials you provide. In order to do this you must do your market research. You need to know how your work compares with other stores in your area.

Turn-Around-Time

We live in an instant society. My generation grew up on instant cereal, instant pudding, and Polaroid's instant pictures. We now have photocopy machines for instant printing, faxes, e-mail, and beepers. Drive-through services have expanded from banks and fast food to where some jewelry stores have them to pick up repairs.

We want it NOW – NOW – NOW!

We do want it now, and we realize there is a price to pay to have it now. That price is in either higher cost or lower quality. Your customers for shop services are no different.

Prices

One store that I tried to gain as a new account for my trade shop told me they could not send their repair work to me because my prices were too high. I sat down with the owner of that store with their retail price list. Many of their retail prices were less than my wholesale prices, and indeed, they would lose money using me as a source.

I went over their cost of doing repairs in-house with the storeowner. Every time a repair job was performed in their store, they lost money because their prices were so low. This storeowner informed me he could not raise his prices, he had to accept the losses in his shop because of the market in his area. All the other stores in town were that low. If he raised his prices, he would lose business.

Unknown to this jeweler, the store down the street was an account of mine. They sent their repair work to me and keystoned my prices. They were getting two to three times the amount for their repair work as this store was getting. The first store was afraid to raise their prices because they thought they would price themselves higher than all the other stores in town. When in fact many of the other stores in town were two to three times higher than their prices.

Customers

Finally, you must look at what the Market Will Bear. What the market will bear has nothing to do with what other stores charge. Unless you are a trade-shop the other stores are NOT your market – They Are Your Competition.

Your market is your customers, the people you sell to. Knowing the maximum they will pay is knowing what the market will bear. This is the most important consideration in setting your prices. What are YOUR CUSTOMERS Willing To Pay?

Often our customers are willing to pay more for our repairs than we are charging. Knowing how much you can raise your prices will allow you to maximize your profits in the shop.

An excellent method to use is to compare what your customers willingly pay for other similar services and then price your services correspondingly. For example, the ladies that shop at your store gets their hair done every month or so. Find out what they pay to have their hair cut & styled and you can set your ring sizing prices accordingly.

If you don't believe that they will be willing to pay you the same to size their ring as they are paying their Beautician to have their hair styled or their nails manicured, then you are in the wrong business!

Setting Your Price

To set your prices you must first figure your cost on each repair. This Cost Based Price should be seen as a pricing floor. This is the lowest possible price you can charge for an item or service. Charging less than this will result in losing money.

Next, determine the maximum the market will bear. This is the price ceiling. Customers will not pay more than this price on a consistent basis. Between the two is the "Room" for your pricing. Then, knowing your position in the industry, set your price somewhere in this room, between the floor and the ceiling.

Setting your prices in this "room" allows you to set your prices properly for your store. By doing so, you will maximize the profits on each repair. Workflow will increase from the additional customers bringing repairs to you because your prices are set fairly. Resulting in a more profitable store for you.

Above all, Price Fairly – neither too high nor too low. If you charge too little, you will not make a profit. You might even loose business because clients will think there is something wrong with your work. However, if you charge too much, you will likely be turned down for work (at least repeat work) and clients probably will not tell you why.

If you regret having to perform the repair work on a particular job, then your prices are probably too low. However, if a customer does not leave their jewelry for you to repair and you feel the work could have been done for less. Then your prices are probably too high. Always set your prices so that you are happy to do the work if the customer leaves their jewelry with you and just as happy if they do not. Knowing that you will be paid fairly for your efforts and that you could not make any money performing the work for less. If you can be content in both of these situations – Then you have set your prices properly for your store.

Overcoming the BIGGEST Obstacle to Raising Prices

Brad Simon

I have found that whenever we raised jewelry repair prices in any of the stores I worked for, repairs would drop off for about 6 months. I always thought we might have raised our prices too high, and customers were objecting to the prices. Then one day we implemented a substantial price increase and shop work really dropped off. I asked the salespeople concerning this as it was really affecting the shop's income. I asked them how many customers were turning down repair work because the price was too high. They told me NONE!

What I found out was that the SALESPEOPLE thought the price was too high not the customers. When a customer brought a ring in to be sized in the past, they would recommend other add-on repairs like retipping. Now, because they thought the price was too high they were afraid to ask for addition work. I even found salespeople recommend putting on a gold-filled ring guard instead of sizing down because they were afraid to ask for the higher price. After about 6 months the salespeople became accustom to the new prices and the repair work would be back to normal.

To me the biggest hurdle to overcome in raising prices is the salesperson not the customers! How can we charge so much for jewelry repair, when the customer has so many needs? The salespeople would ask. It is easier to charge more for a perceived 'need' than a 'want', they would reason, and jewelry repair and custom design is just a 'want' not a 'need'.

I agree, charging for needs is easier than charging for a want. However, you have to realize that jewelry and jewelry repairs is not a want, a desire, or a luxury – IT IS A NEED!

Remember back in school we learned about Maslow's Hierarchy of Needs. Abraham Maslow developed a list of humans' five needs. The first is Physical Needs. These are the basic needs like air, food, water, and sleep. Next is Safety / Security Needs followed by Social Needs. The fourth on the list is Esteem Needs. These needs involve achievement, status, and self-respect. Once the lower needs are met, people have a NEED to have their self-esteem built up. Just because it is not a basic need does not make it any less of a need. Most people meet this need with status symbols such as cars, homes, vacations, or electronic gadgets, and many meet the need with JEWELRY. Not everyone meets this need with jewelry, but most of the people who darken our door do so to have that need fulfilled with jewelry. The customer that comes to us with a ring to be sized NEEDS that ring to fit so that they can wear it. It is not a want -- it is a need!

We must realize that just because jewelry and our custom/repair services meet a higher level need, it is still a NEED. It is just as much of a need as the food we eat and the air we breathe. Jewelry is not a want, a desire, or a luxury it is a need. It is a need just as real as hunger, thirst, or a physical injury. When we can understand this need in our customers and see how we can fulfill it, we will then be able to overcome our objection to quoting higher prices.

Shop Safety

Quote Worth Re-Quoting

"Working safely may get old, but so do those who practice it.

Safety doesn't happen by Accident."

— Author Unknown

A Pain In The Neck

Brad Simon

You turn and there it is. You get up from your chair and it happens again. That nagging pain in your neck or lower back. After several years at the bench, one often develops chronic neck or back injuries.

Bench jewelers will spend most of the time in the workshop seated at their workbench. Therefore, time is well spent in adjusting the seating arrangement. A poorly adjusted chair and workbench will not only cause discomfort, fatigue, and muscle cramps, reducing worker efficiency, but more importantly, it may develop into leg, back, or neck injury.

Many varieties of workbench styles are available from jewelry tool and equipment suppliers. Unfortunately, almost all benches come in a standard height of 39" to 40" and are not adjustable. This one size fits all bench height, fits worse than one-size fits all clothing. Since jewelers are not all the same height, the workbench MUST be adjusted to fit them.

Adjusting Your Chair

To achieve the proper workbench height you must first start with the chair. A jeweler may sit in their chair for over eight hours per day, every day, and even longer during the Christmas Season. A quality chair made for sitting for long periods and ergonomically designed is necessary. Your body, limbs, spine, and neck will be supported by and affected by the chair you sit in. Pain associated with seating may develop slowly, often over many months or even years. A good chair will go a long way toward preventing these problems.

When selecting a chair do not be fooled by the visual appearance. For example, a soft, overly padded chair may look inviting and when you sit in it for the first few moments, it may feel comfortable and soothing. Over an eight-hour workday, however, this chair may not support your back, legs, and spine properly.

Once you have purchased a chair, you must adjust it. The best chair in the world is worthless if it is not adjusted correctly.

Adjust the height of the chair so that when seated with feet flat on the floor the tops of your thighs are parallel to the floor. You should be able to feel the seat of the chair along the back of your thighs. You should feel enough pressure to support your upper legs, but not too much pressure as to cut off or restrict circulation. The angle between the torso and the thighs should not be less than 90° or greater than 110°. From this position, you need to adjust the height of the workbench. DO NOT adjust the height of the chair to the workbench.

A chair too high is awkward for shorter jewelers, and it is hard to reach the foot pedal for the flex shaft. It puts pressure on the thighs, restricting circulation in the legs. Improper support of the legs and thighs lead to chronic back injury.

A chair too low is uncomfortable for taller jewelers. Their knees are raised too high, eliminating any support of their thighs. This causes compression of the lower spine and body organs. Alternatively, they bend their legs awkwardly under them, causing fatigue and cramping. Both lead to chronic back injury.

A backrest on the chair is necessary to help support the spine. The backrest should support the lower and middle of your back, from your waist to just below your shoulder blades. Less than this does not give adequate support, more than this restricts movement.

Adjust the backrest up or down to give this support. Then adjust the backrest forward or backwards so that there is 2" to 4" of clearance between the front edge of the seat and the inside of your knees. Just like your thighs against the chair seat, you should be able to feel the support of the chair backrest along your back. While sitting, your spine is supported either by a backrest or by your muscles. Avoid fatigue from muscular backache and get a chair with a properly adjusted backrest.

Adjusting Your Bench

To determine the proper workbench height, sit comfortably in a properly adjusted chair. Sit up straight with your back against the backrest. In this position, your bench pin should come to the center of your breastbone. If it does not, you need to adjust the height of your bench. Buying the proper chair and adjusting it correctly will do you no good if you hunch over your work because your bench is too short!

If your bench is too tall, you can cut the required amount off each leg. Be certain to cut exactly the same amount off each leg so that the bench does not wobble. If the bench is too short, glue a block of wood to the bottom of each leg to raise the bench.

Visors

Many magnifying visors available in the jewelry industry hold the magnifying lens plate out directly in front of your eyes. This forces you to look straight ahead, not down at your work. To see your work on your bench pin you must bend over your work. This also leads to chronic back and neck injury.

Many jewelers further complicate this problem when someone comes to talk to them while working. Rather than raise the visor, they bend their necks back and look down under the visor to see the person. Over time, a jeweler develops a whiplash type injury from this extreme bending of the neck.

A better alternative is to use a magnifier that sets lower in front of the eyes, such as reading glasses. To use, you look down through the glasses and only need to bend your head forward slightly, if at all. Then to see someone you can look straight out over the glasses without bending your neck.

Chiropractor

Last, but certainly not least, visit a chiropractor. Find a chiropractor that works with occupational injuries and provides maintenance care. Chiropractors that only work with acute injuries (such as auto accidents) may not be as proficient at working with chronic injury that bench jewelers develop. In addition, find a chiropractor that will take x-rays of your spine before making any adjustments. Any competent chiropractor will want to see just what condition your spine is in before making adjustments.

By making a few ergonomic adjustments to your shop, changing some bad work habits, as well as receiving chiropractic maintenance, your back will begin to feel as good as new and you will have one less Pain In The Neck!

Organizing the Messes

Charles Lewton-Brian

How you set up your shop, your working procedures and workspace can affect your safety, comfort, stress level and efficiency of making and repairing jewelry. If your shop is well planned, you will be more efficient. The more efficient you are, the faster you work and the more creative time you will have available to you. It pays to spend some time on organization.

The more you think about and plan your workspace and what you do in it the easier life as a craftsperson will be for you. And it's safer, too. Many accidents happen because equipment is badly positioned, or there is clutter. Avoid making piles or having things too messy. Be smart in how you set up your space. It is important to set aside the time to describe and analyze what you do in your craft so that you can see better how to improve things.

Draw a Map of Your Workplace.

It helps to make a plan of your workshop, like an architect's view of the layout of a floor in a house. Make it fairly big to have room to make notes on it. Draw in walls for the rooms and list on it the various jobs that are done in different areas. Label major equipment on the drawing. Draw in arrows to show how workpieces flow through the shop from entry to exit. Do some cross-hatching on it to identify areas where hazardous materials are stored and use some different kind of marking to show where hazardous noise is encountered.

Indicate with X's where ergonomic dangers may be present. Mark where space usage and access issues are present. Then add to your blossoming drawing little triangles to indicate where there are airborne hazards. Finally, make little colored stick-on dots where accidents or near accidents have occurred in the past, this will show where accident clusters happen. Accidents happen less often if things are tidy and organized.

Now look at your plan and see if you can rearrange jobs or equipment to make things a little safer, more efficient, productive and easier to live in. Think about access, ergonomics, confined spaces, traffic flow, fire dangers, extinguisher placement and all the issues above.

Segregate different jobs, that have specific workstations for different jobs. Chemical use, for instance should be done in a fume hood. Remember proper ventilation in your shop is vital. It helps to have low isolating walls around workstations to keep processes separate and hence more controllable in safety terms.

It is a good idea to have your office in a separate room from your workshop. This is to lower your overall exposure to your workshop materials and processes. I knew someone who fried their computer's mother board in a combined office/workshop space because enough minuscule metallic dust entered it causing it to short circuit.

The workstation should be carefully designed to be efficient, allow ease of work and to be safe. Tools get positioned around the workstation for maximum accessibility in order of frequency of use. Have tools in rotating bins, or blocks with tools sprouting from them that move about the work surface, use shelves, open compartments and tool boards.

Easy reach and avoidance of twisting motions to reach tools are important considerations. An example of the effects of a workstation alteration is switching to a telephone headset. Users don't hurt their necks or jaws and are up to 48% more efficient at getting work done.

Look for role models that you can learn from. Look for others who must work smoothly, accurately, safely. And rapidly. How about doctors, surgeons, dentists, and tattooists?

All your tools should be laid out in a manner that fits the way they are used. Each one to have a place and every tool kept in its place. As one gets older, phrases like "put things back where you found them" begin to make more sense. Just like a chemistry lab, try and have most table surfaces empty much of the time.

Spend some time analyzing your shop and discuss the results with someone knowledgeable. You will find you work easier, happier and faster.

Workshop Safety Tips

Charles Lewton-Brian

The first thought on having an accident is usually -**That Was Stupid!**

At least for me and from others who I have asked, the first thought that goes through your head, even before anything hurts, is that was dumb. And, usually, it was. Most accidents (including the slow ones that get you twenty years down the line) are stupid ones. In the light of the best knowledge at your disposal (and it is your duty to yourself to do the research to find out about what you are doing) act in such a manner as to avoid accidents and threats to your health.

Be smart, work calmly and steadily, think and be conscious.

Give Yourself A Grade

I am a teacher, and one of the things I do when I grade my students is to be as objective as possible. I take into account their individual skills, how much they have personally developed and pushed themselves, how hard they worked and how they excelled against their own goals and aspirations. I do not look at just what they did to fulfill any parameters of the projects I set for them.

This means that I have to judge myself by the same criteria in order to avoid being a hypocrite. As an educator one has to be a sort of role model as a form of continuous education. This can be kind of rough. So, grade yourself in terms of your safety efforts.

There is no shame in a mediocre grade, merely an indication that one can do better. Don't put yourself down for doing your best – that is as good as it gets. So, assuming you are doing your best for yourself then give yourself a grade in that regard. Then try again.

One tends to get better and improve this way. Judge yourself as you would judge another person's performance given the same problem to solve or project to carry out. And give yourself credit. If it is an 'A' grade, then that is what it is. Enjoy!

Safety Equipment

Have lots of personal safety equipment around. We have hooks on the walls of our studio every five feet and on them hang safety glasses, face shields and ear muffs. Make using your safety equipment easy to do. When all you have to do is reach out a hand in any direction to reach safety equipment you will be more likely to use it.

To keep safety glasses scratch free I keep mine in a plastic bag and place them there every time I take them off. If they are scratched, you will be more reluctant to use them. We are used to being somewhat stingy with safety equipment, trying to make it last a long time, accepting an irritation with scratches on the lenses in an attempt to 'save money'. It is better to have your equipment easy to reach and pleasant to use, so you don't have to resent it.

Personal safety equipment like this is an operating cost. Budget for it so you can have good, scratch free glasses and other equipment at hand when you need them.

Rules for Tools

While it is clearly impossible to give a set of rules for each tool and procedure that goldsmiths use, this section gives some examples of the kinds of rules that may be helpful to review when using powered equipment. Hand tools and processes have been left out, primarily because their dangers tend to be of the "don't put your hands in the way of things that might snap or slip" kind.

We have a power rolling mill at the college where I teach. It was felt that it was too dangerous to allow students to use without special training. I had a number of students sit down with me and we created a list of rules for usage, then a question for each of the rules. A student has to get 100% on the test, receive personal instruction and be watched by an instructor before they get their name on a list on the wall allowing them to use the mill.

It helps to have a rule set for a piece of equipment. This can seem like quite a lot to remember, but most of it is very much common sense and only starts to look overwhelming if you write it all down.

There are basic aspects of a common sense approach to working with tools. Don't put yourself or others in danger. This is a really important principle that bears repeating. Work safely electrically, physically, ergonomically, chemically and in terms of dust and exposure to materials altered by using the tool.

Equipment

Equipment should be operated safely and checked periodically for condition and potential hazards. Keep a file of the instruction manuals that came with it and at least once every six months check everything for wear and hazardous conditions.

Because you should have a list of your equipment anyway for insurance purposes you might as well have that list be a log of repairs needed etc. for the equipment. This is an example of combining acts for greater effectiveness – take something you have to do anyway and then make up other reasons to do the same job.

Grinding Wheel Safety Thoughts

Wear adequate eye and hearing protection. Wear hair up and avoid loose clothing or jewelry.

Do not talk to anyone or have any distractions while grinding

Keep this tool in its own small area, free of clutter, preferably with at least low walls around the area to isolate the tool and debris from it.

Have good housekeeping and clean the area around the tool after every use. Clean up particles using hand broom/vacuum (never with your hands) after every use of the machine. Make a habit of it.

Have good lighting on the working area of the wheel, a mounted desk lamp or one on each side is good (illumination from two sides eliminates shadows)

Always have the machine properly mounted and screwed securely in place onto a sturdy work surface.

Turn off the machine when not in use.

Wear fireproof clothing/apron.

Keep all flammable materials such as paper, cloth, solvents, and potential fuels away from the grinding area.

Do not grind wood or other flammable materials on the same wheel used for metals.

Always use a wheel guard.

When starting a grinder always stand safely to one side until the wheel has reached speed and run for a few seconds at speed. If a grinding wheel is going to fly apart it often does so during the wind-up phase.

Use the right grinding wheel for the job, properly rated for the motor speed and the correct size.

Inspect the grinding wheels carefully on a regular basis.

Grind evenly across the face; avoid creating ruts in the wheel.

Dress the wheel with a wheel dressing tool if required to keep a wheel flat. Wheels with chips, flat spots, gouges and glazed areas should be dressed. Bad spots like that can make grinding more hazardous and inefficient, reduce accuracy, and damage the work surface by burning or gouging it. Dressing your wheel helps keep it balanced, which is important for safety.

Always keep the tool rest the correct distance from the wheel, usually 1/16th of an inch (1.5 mm). As the wheel is ground down the tool rest needs to be reset.

Have a water dip next to the wheel; small water pans designed for this can be attached to the front and middle of the grinder. Dip frequently to cool the workpiece. Always cool a workpiece before putting it down and picking up the next one.

Dust collectors

Sometimes jewelers use dust collection systems intended for wood working on their polishing machines. This is fine as long as you don't mix woodworking activities and metal working ones. I've seen a local ventilation hose from a big belt sander catch fire when sparks from grinding metal ignited wood dust in the hose. I've seen polishing machine filters catch on fire twice from sparks thrown into them, once a nickel silver neckpiece that was caught on the wheel and once from sanding steel.

The Dead Man's Switch

Really bad, scary, wicked machines in industry have a 'dead man's switch'. This is a device that the worker has to activate in order to use the machine. Unless it is pressed there is no power to the machine.

Ideally in order to use the machine the workers hands and body are kept safe because they are operating the switch. If there is an accident the worker automatically releases the switch and the power to the machine is immediately cut off.

A relative of this is a power cutoff in the form of a foot pedal, usually housed inside a hood so that one cannot accidentally tread on it and activate it. One has to consciously insert the foot into the housing to press down on the foot pedal thus giving power to the machine. If one releases the foot pedal or pulls the foot out of the housing the machine is shut down. We have one on the power rolling mill at the college I teach at.

I think that polishing motors are a really good candidate for foot operated cutoff switches like this.

Eyes

Aside from protection from sharp objects, flying chunks of metal, dust, splashes, and chemicals, we have to deal with glowing materials (infrared light), the blue flame of a high temperature torch (ultraviolet light) and 'sodium glare'. These are the three kinds of non-ionizing radiation that we worry about.

Good quality eye protection against infrared radiation is recommended. Most glasses and polycarbonates will stop the ultraviolet. The infrared is stopped by a 'shade', a number 2 and up has been suggested by a welding institute source. It is important that one understands that a "tinted' lens does not offer infrared protection – only a shaded lens offers protection.

Glasses and Contacts

Polycarbonate glasses are much more shatter resistant than regular glass. There are reports of glasses shattering upon impact. There are also reports of bits of plastic or polycarbonate flying into the eyes if the frames are bent to try and fit when they are too small for the head.

If you wear glasses you can have safety glasses with safety frames made at the optometrist which are prescription, bifocal, or whatever you need. Some metalworkers wear polycarbonate safety glass over their regular glasses. "There are many different styles of safety glasses that will fit over prescription glasses".

It is advisable to have safety glasses with side shields to protect against things bouncing in from the side of the head. They should also fit well, particularly at the brow.

From everything I have read and heard it is not a good idea to wear contacts in a jewelry shop. The dust and chemicals can get stuck under the contact and scratch the eye, some fumes can permeate certain contacts.

**We only have two of them,
so we need to take care of our eyes.**

Work Clothing

There is a reason that people in factories wear work clothing. It is safer. Cotton is a good choice. I was once grinding a vise in a craft school workshop and was using a lab coat from the shop (which I assumed was an appropriate one) while using an angle grinder. I noticed a burning smell and looked down to find that there was a spreading pool of flames on my stomach – the lab coat was a nylon one and very flammable. Unthinkingly I patted the flames out only to have molten lava – like plastic well up through my fingers making the burn a really bad one in between the fingers. Make sure all your clothing is flame resistant in a jewelry shop.

Don't ever wear sandals or bare feet (several bad stories about folks ramming needles, sawblades etc. deep into their toes). Steel toed shoes are a good idea (I've met more than one person who has dropped a stake or other object on a toe and broken it). Good, protective footwear in the studio is always recommended.

And most important, using work clothes such as an apron, overalls or a jump suit helps keep chemicals and metal residues in the work shop and out of the rest of your life, and your family's life. Work clothing should be washed regularly and separately from other laundry.

Metals

Our bodies react to metals, their dusts, salts and oxides. We need certain amounts of most metals in our bodies – but not too little or too much.

Metals have 'concentration windows', that means that too little contact may be damaging and too much is really damaging. The exposure window can be very small in some cases – it is easy to have too much contact with some metals.

Of note is that exposure to multiple metals can result in interactions between them which result in greater damage than exposure to a single metal alone. An example is the interaction of cadmium and zinc or the ability of lead to displace calcium (a metal) and thus affect the nervous system.

One of the concerns is self-dosing of metals in the form of supplements, there have been several cases of chrome poisoning from this. Have a look at what you are consciously ingesting as well.

Again, you are exposed to metals by touching them, breathing or ingesting their oxides and dusts and at higher temperatures their fumes. The worst metals to have around include cadmium, nickel, antimony, beryllium

Fumes, Vapor & Mist

Fumes are small particles of a material, often from metals that have been melted. These may be very tiny and can be breathed into the lungs. Metal fume fever is a real hazard with molten metals. It has numerous names, the nastiest of which is 'the smothers'.

Metal fume fever can be caused by zinc, copper, magnesium, aluminum, copper, antimony, cadmium, iron, and silver. The particles are so small (0.01-0/5 microns) that they stay in the air a long time. Because they are so tiny, they go deeper into your lungs and can then dissolve more easily within your body.

I have known a number of people to experience metal fume fever, from zinc while casting or reticulating brass and once from copper, because they did not use adequate ventilation. Casting brass is a particular culprit, often because ventilation is frequently a hood type above a casting machine and the fumes are then drawn past the workers face on their way out. So, don't cast brass unless you can help it, use very good ventilation when melting or reticulating metals, and if you must do it then use the correct respirator.

You get vapors when you turn a liquid into a gas, for example as water evaporates to make water vapor. The vapors jewelers worry about most are from solvents, acids and simmering solutions. Remember that things can vaporize at room temperature – even frozen sheets will dry on the line in the cold. Mercury vaporizes at room temperature.

Mists are small droplets of chemicals in liquid form. If one quenches into a pickle pot for instance a mist is formed. It has been shown that in factory situations people exposed to mists of sulfuric acid develop pitted enamel in their teeth. Mists are more toxic than vapors because they deliver a more concentrated solution to spots in the lungs and elsewhere.

Chemicals

If you know what the chemicals are that you use and what their dangers are you will be less likely to hurt yourself with them. You should have a list of the chemicals in your workshop (a chemical inventory), MSDS sheets and chemical profile sheets which tell you important information about the chemical.

A chemical profile sheet is theoretically easier to read than a standard MSDS sheet. There are several places on the internet where chemical profiles are available. One is http://nsc.org/ehc/ew/chemical.htm.

Mishandling of chemicals is the main cause of accidents with them: spills, accidental reactions, contamination, breathing, etc. Because so many products contain chemicals, you should ideally have information for every product in your workshop that contains chemicals, as well as those clearly identifiable ones that you think of immediately when one says chemical.

DERMATITIS

Dermatitis is a group of skin conditions that may often be contracted by exposure to chemicals and metals. It is a real hazard for jewelers. I once knew someone whose dermatitis got so bad that her hands would begin to crack and bleed when she walked into a jewelry studio and she had to give it up, in her fourth year of school.

Working unsafely, dipping fingers into solvents, cutting oils for lapidary, mixing investments with bare hands and so on defat the skin which then loses its protection against other chemicals and metals. Moving to mechanical cleaning methods (scotch brite scrubbing) to reduce chemical (soaps-even the mild ones) exposure can help as well.

It has been suggested not to wear a ring in the workshop because dusts and chemicals tend to get caught under the ring and then react with the skin more easily; as well as getting caught on things.

Fire Safety

Last but not least have a fire plan! Ask your fire department for advice. Keep the appropriate extinguishers around and in good shape. Mount them near exits.

Bench Magazine Series of Instructional Guidebooks

Available at:
BenchMagazine.com & Amazon.com

Guide to Stonesetting

Setting Gemstones in jewelry is one of the more demanding tasks a Bench Jeweler faces. This book is designed to help jewelers develop and improve their stonesetting skills.

Here you will discover all about setting gemstones in gold and platinum jewelry. You'll learn fundamental setting procedures as well as advanced techniques. Short tips and tricks as well as full length articles on various techniques that can help you improve your stonesetting skills.

Guide to Jewelry Making

Creating a piece of jewelry by hand is a mark of true craftsmanship. This book goes beyond the basics and teaches jewelry making techniques that will stretch your creativity. From Basic Techniques to Advanced Applications - From Centuries Old Procedures to the Latest in Technological Advancements,

Here you will discover jewelry making techniques others use to succeed. Whether you are a beginning jeweler looking to make your own jewelry, develop your jewelry making skills, and build your career as a jeweler or a seasoned veteran of the bench looking to refresh your skills and rejuvenate your career, Bench Magazine's Guide to Jewelry Making will help jump-start your creativity and motivate you to accomplish your goals.

Guide to Jewelry Repair

Discover how you can improve the quality of your work and increase productivity in the shop while performing everyday repairs. Traditional Torch Methods as well as Modern Processes utilizing Laser Welders and Electro Welders are all covered.

Numerous Bench Tips and Tricks are presented throughout the book by the various Master Jewelers. Plus a special section of Favorite Tips is included. From sizing rings & chain repair to advanced jewelry repair, the articles in this book are designed to help jewelers develop and improve their skills and provide the information you need to create a more efficient jewelry shop.

Guide to Bench Tips

Working at the Bench encompasses only a few basic techniques. However, there are numerous tips and tricks to use in mastering those techniques. Discover what works and what doesn't from our experienced Master Jewelers, and learn about the Tools, Techniques, Tips, and Tricks others use to succeed.

This book offers a wide selection of tips and tricks presented by Working Master Jewelers to provide you the knowledge to help you improve your skills and add new techniques to make your services more valuable to your customers and employer.

Additional Shop Management Books by Bench Media

Available at:
BenchMagazine.com & Amazon.com

Run Your Shop Without It Running You
by Brad Simon

A Practical Guide To Efficient Shop Management

With over one hundred and fifty pages of information, illustrations, and worksheets, this is the most comprehensive book on Shop Management available today. Discover a variety of methods to improve profitability of the jewelry shop. Including; how to set correct prices, improve scrap material management, and avoiding costly mistakes at the take-in counter.

In Addition, you'll discover methods of increasing productivity without sacrificing quality. Including; organizing and scheduling jobs, shop design, organizing the bench, motivating the bench jeweler, and many other topics.

This Valuable Guide Is A Must In Every Retail Jewelry Store

It's About Time
by Brad Simon

A Practical Guide to Increasing Productivity in the Jewelry Repair Shop.

Discover how you can increase productivity without sacrificing the quality of your work through time management and organizational principals designed for the creative minded bench jeweler.

"Productivity was up 18% companywide in the first month after implementing your ideas on productivity." Helzberg Diamonds

"We had a great Christmas season, if it wasn't for your scheduling & organization information, I don't know how we would have gotten all the work done." Mike Peterson

"Very practical advice, it's well thought out." John Caro

Made in the USA
Columbia, SC
18 April 2023